D1084395

Applied Hypnosis:
An Overview

Applied Hypnosis:
An Overview

Benjamin Wallace

Nelson-Hall nh Chicago

Library of Congress Cataloging in Publication Data

Wallace, Benjamin.
  Applied hypnosis.
  Bibliography: p.
  Includes indexes.
  1. Hypnotism—Therapeutic use. I. Title.
[DNLM: 1. Hypnosis—Popular works. WM415.3 W187a]
RC495.W27   615'.8512   79-65
ISBN 0-88229-415-6

Copyright © 1979 by Benjamin Wallace

Manufactured in the United States of America

10   9   8   7   6   5   4   3   2   1

To my lovely wife, Roni

Contents

Acknowledgments

I WOULD LIKE to express my gratitude to Drs. James Garrett, Thomas Guest, and Ian Wickramasekera for reading and beneficially commenting on drafts of various chapters of this book. I also would like to thank Roni Wallace for helping me make the book more readable and Jo Gibson, Karen Nelson, Jody Shryack Glynn, and Lucia Beck Weiss for helping with various stages of typing and proofreading the manuscript.

Preface

STUDENTS AND LAYMEN often have asked if I could recommend
a book to them on the topic of hypnosis which they could read
in a relatively short period of time and which they could easily
comprehend. I have explained to them that generally two types
of books are available. The first includes what is referred to as
the popularized paperback. In most instances these rather in-
expensive books are written for the layman *by the layman*.
Their faults are readily apparent. They exhibit a paucity of research documentation concerning topics covered and are
replete with simplistic statements, inaccuracies, and sensationalized half-truths. Furthermore, this type of book contains
neither a subject index nor a list of additional readings for
those interested in delving beyond the scope of the book.
Therefore, I have explained to inquirers that I could not recommend such a book to them.

The second type of book available on the topic of hypnosis is highly technical in nature and has been written by a sci-
entist for the scientific community. Although this type of book
easily qualifies as an excellent and well-documented source of
information, the average reader would have extreme difficulty
understanding many of the concepts contained and elaborated

on in such a text. Therefore, I have felt that this type of text also would not meet the needs of my inquirers.

Thus, I have been forced to admit that I could not recommend a book from either category that would be scientifically accurate, yet easy to comprehend and quick to read. As a result of having to respond in this fashion for the past five years, I decided that I could best serve the needs of future students and laymen by writing such a book myself.

I felt the best approach would be to concentrate on the applied aspects of hypnosis, as most inquirers seem to be interested in how hypnosis works and how it might benefit them and others. The result is *Applied Hypnosis*.

Each chapter of the book is written in a professional and scientifically documented manner, but in language as nontechnical as possible. Where technical jargon could not be avoided, terms used are carefully defined. The concentration of the book is on the known, applied uses of hypnosis in today's society. Each chapter concentrates on a major aspect of applied hypnosis. In addition, comparisons of hypnosis with alternative behavioral change techniques are made throughout, so that the reader can determine if hypnosis is more beneficial for use in a given area of concern. The book also contains a simple, self-administered hypnotic susceptibility scale to permit the reader to determine in a brief period of time whether he or she is readily hypnotizable.

All in all, this book should help fill a gap in the literature, providing a much-needed information source on applied hypnosis for the student and the layman. As such, it offers important and unique features traditionally unavailable to the person who asks, "Can you recommend a good book on hypnosis to me?"

Introduction

A QUESTION OFTEN asked by professionals and laymen alike is, "What is hypnosis?" Is it the mystical, magical ability to make people do what you tell them to do even against their own will? Or is it something that can be explained in a scientific manner, independent of such uncertainties as magic or mystery? It may seem unusual to begin a book on hypnosis by asking these questions; however, one reason for doing so is that a definition of this phenomenon is as controversial as the phenomenon itself.

Some researchers define hypnosis as a trance state characterized by a very relaxed, drowsy, and lethargic appearance (Conn and Conn, 1967; Fromm and Shor, 1972; Hilgard, 1965; Shor and Orne, 1965). During this trance state the person who has been hypnotized loses initiative to carry out his own plans, redirects his attention away from the activity in which he was engaged toward the instructions of the hypnotist, has a heightened ability to produce fantasies, and has an increased susceptibility to suggestions (Hilgard, 1965).

Another definition of hypnosis does not include the concept of a trance state. Instead, hypnosis is characterized as behavior resulting from positive attitudes, strong motivations,

1

and positive, enhanced expectancies toward the situation in which the subject finds himself (Barber, Spanos and Chaves, 1974). Consequently, subjects are willing to follow the suggestions of the hypnotist.

Whether one accepts the trance explanation or the cognitive-behavioral explanation of the hypnotic phenomenon, one thing is certain: during hypnosis subjects appear capable of demonstrating many abilities typically not possible in a normal, waking state.

How was the phenomenon of hypnosis discovered? One of the earliest reported instances of a process resembling hypnosis can be traced to a Viennese physician named Friedrich Anton Mesmer (1734-1815). In 1774, mesmerism (the original name for hypnosis) was demonstrated by Mesmer with the aid of magnetic plates which had been invented by a Jesuit priest and astronomy professor named Father Hell. The purpose of these plates was to induce so-called cosmic fluids to react in individuals. This reaction was called animal magnetism. The process was begun by placing metal bottles of water in a large wooden tub known as a baquet. These bottles had been magnetized previously by Mesmer. The bottles were placed in the tub on a surface of powdered glass and iron filings. Then the tub was filled with water and covered with a lid containing openings through which passed iron rods of varying lengths, which were applied to parts of an individual's body. Patients were seated around this magnetic field, holding each other's hands and their own iron rods. Often the mesmerist would apply his hands to the patient's body, as this was believed to enhance the effect. In addition, mesmerism frequently was performed within the confines of a dimly lit and quiet room.

When mesmeric states were induced in individuals, they exhibited convulsions, fits, and seizures. These reactions were believed to have been due to several factors: the subject's self-expectancy for such convulsions; the release of anxiety obtainable from voluntary seizures; and the fashionable fits commonly exhibited by society women during this era (Shor, 1972). Mesmer professed to cure many afflictions with the use of his powers—afflictions ranging in severity from minor aches and pains to blindness in certain cases.

Owing to the mystical and extremely unorthodox methods of altering behavior and behavioral disorders with the use ̇of mesmerism, the scientific and medical communities decided not to associate themselves with animal magnetism. Later, however, the Marquis de Puyṣegur (1780s) discovered that during the mesmeric process a state of artificial somnambulism, or a sleep-like trance, was present in patients. With the revelation of the presence of a trance state, the entire focus of mesmerism shifted away from the convulsive crisis state, believed by Mesmer to be the basis of the "cure" from the magnetic process. With this new centering of concern on artificial somnambulism, mesmerism began to become scientifically sophisticated and, therefore, more acceptable to some members of the scientific community.

In an examination of the somnambulistic state, Puysegur observed that mesmerized subjects could remain in such a state with their eyes open or closed, could communicate freely with the mesmerist, and would respond easily to the mesmerist's suggestions. The animal magnetism which Mesmer believed necessary to bring about his induced, altered state of consciousness was found to be totally unnecessary. It so happens that Mesmer had realized early in his career that a state of somnambulism was evident during a mesmeric induction, but as this state was irrelevant to the production of the convulsive crises, he considered it only as an interruption of and a side consequence to the therapeutic process. The consequences of the historic shift away from animal magnetism and the willful control of physical, mystical cosmic fluids toward the notion that suggestion from the mesmerist to the patient produced behavioral change led to widespread experimentation with mesmerically induced trance states.

In the 1830s, John Elliotson (1791-1868), a professor of medicine at University College in London, was developing interest in mesmerism and had tried to gain consent to give clinical lectures on the topic to medical students. During that era this task was as difficult as trying to obtain legalization rights for alcohol had been during the Prohibition period in the United States. His colleagues refused to witness any of his demonstrations and were annoying and obnoxious in their rejection of him. In 1837, the university of his affiliation even passed a formal resolution forbidding him to practice mesmerism within the confines of the hospital. This was a professional insult to Elliotson and he soon resigned his post. Later (1843) he began publishing the *Zoist*, a journal of "cerebral physiology and mesmerism" which continued in press until 1856 when its mission of publishing accounts of hypnosis and distributing them to the scientific community had been accomplished.

Meanwhile in India, James Esdaile (1808-1859) also was practicing and advocating the use of mesmerism in some medical and therapeutic situations. Fortunately for Esdaile, the "mesmeric climate" was far better in India than it was for Elliotson in England. The British government in India proved to be far more open-minded than the medical profession in either India or England. Esdaile's mesmerism practices were so successful in alleviating many symptoms in patients that in 1846 the government helped him establish a small hospital devoted to the use of mesmerism as a tool in treating patients. One common use of hypnosis was as an anesthetic during surgery.

Subsequent to the somnambulistic era of Puysegur and around the time of Elliotson, a theory of considerable importance to the history of hypnosis was formulated by James Braid, an English surgeon, in his book *Neurypnology* (1843). Braid recognized that certain mesmeric phenomena were genuine, but rejected, as had Puysegur before him, all mesmeric theories of external influences. Taking as his starting point the eye fixation induction technique that he had observed in demonstrations by the mesmerist Lafontaine, Braid advanced a naturalistic, physiological explanation. He theorized that a staring fixation on a bright object for a given period induced fatigue of the levator muscles of the eyelids, which in turn promoted a general exhaustion of the nerve centers.

A few years later Braid changed the name of mesmerism to neur-hypnotism. (Later the prefix was dropped.) This very change in name helped to considerably alter mesmerism's public and professional image. Because "hypnotism" had a physiological ring to it, the phenomenon could more easily be brought within the bounds of cautious, respectable science.

Three decades later (1870s) a neurological theory of hypnosis was proposed by Jean Martin Charcot. He described hypnotism as consisting of distinct sequential physiological reflex stages in hysterically predisposed individuals. These stages were induced and terminated by certain physical stimuli. Despite the fact that there was not, and still is not, any physiological or other type of evidence to support Charcot's claims, and despite the overall weakness of his theory, his eminence as one of the world's leading neurologists, his rigorous methodology, and his precise neurological descriptions removed many doubts in the medical profession about the scientific respectability of studying hypnotism.

During Charcot's period it was recognized that hypnotism was essentially psychological in nature (neither physiological as Charcot originally had stressed nor in the realm of magic or mysticism as earlier skeptical scientists had classified it). Following this new recognition of the nature of hypnosis, Jose Custodi di Faria stressed that "lucid sleep" (somnambulism) was produced solely by the subject's heightened expectations and receptive attitude.

One expression of di Faria's new psychological outlook was the use in his induction procedure of soothing and commanding verbal suggestions. Mesmer's induction procedures had been based on direct physical contacts that were designed to promote the flow of cosmic fluid in the receptive patient. Thus, the mesmeric process was basically nonverbal. Only when it was recognized that suggestibility played the major role in the mesmeric induction procedure did words become important elements in the process.

Following di Faria, Braid's interests shifted away from theories of rather mechanical, physiological changes in exhausted nervous centers, toward events at the psychological level of analysis. Braid developed a concept which he called monoideism. This referred to an attention-getting process in which the patient focused on a single idea, a single train of thought. For a given period of time, attention was focused on this thought only, while all other thoughts and ideas were attenuated. In this way monoideism heightened the intensity of a dominant idea. This sometimes served to make the subject more easily influenced by hypnotic suggestions. Braid reported that this heightened state of suggestibility could be achieved by only about 10 percent of his subjects.

After Braid's work was translated into French, Ambroise Auguste Liebeault, in 1864, helped establish the so-called doctrine of suggestion. Simply stated, hypnosis was seen as an extension of suggestibility that began by having the subject focus on the idea of sleep. During the ensuing sleep, a suggestion was initiated by the hypnotist and was retained at a conscious level by the subject. This established the necessary support and rapport between the subject and the hypnotist. Thus, ordinary waking suggestibility was seen to result from a temporary inability of the subject to focus on any thought or idea except one suggested by the hypnotist.

While visiting Liebeault's clinic, Sigmund Freud made the fundamental observation that determined the direction of his life's work. He noted that a suggestion given during hypnosis often would not be available to recall upon awakening. The forgotten suggestion, however, could be carried out posthypnotically, with the patient rationalizing reasons for his act. As a result, Freud was led to believe that much human behavior was, in fact, the result of unconscious motivation.

In the meantime Josef Breuer, an older colleague of Freud's, had discovered that the root causes of hysteric symptoms were painful memories and pent-up emotions, buried below consciousness. The hysteric symptoms could be eliminated in an indirect manner by encouraging spontaneous verbalization by patients under hypnosis, to evoke a catharsis of the pent-up energies causing the symptoms.

Freud's development of psychoanalysis began, somewhat paradoxically, with his rejection of hypnotism as his scientific and therapeutic method; however, he never lost interest in developing a theoretical understanding of hypnosis. His abandonment of hypnosis as a therapeutic method was a wise decision, if not a historic necessity, since the authority and obedience brand of hypnotism that dominated his era was too unwieldly and artifact-laden. Hypnotism, moreover, allowed access to certain repressed material too quickly; it suppressed symptoms too easily; and the hypnotized individual's responses were swayed too readily by demand characteristics (Orne, 1962), or what the subject perceived the hypnotist wanted him to do.

Modern hypnotherapy as we know it today can be traced to Milton H. Erickson. In 1923, while still an undergraduate and medical student at the University of Wisconsin, Erickson was invited by Clark Hull to present a graduate seminar on his fascinating informal researches in hypnotism. These events not only marked the beginning of Erickson's productive career, but also, in all likelihood, they helped spark Hull's contributions to hypnotism as well (Hull, 1933).

Briefly stated, Erickson's therapeutic approach emphasizes brevity and limited goals without insight. In dealing with neurosis, for instance, Erickson "enters" the world of the patient's neurosis with him, and rearranges definitions and symptoms to make the neurosis more adaptive. As a result, Erickson's form of hypnotherapy takes the form of a developing relationship between the therapist and his patient who is in an altered state of responsiveness. In this state repressed materials often are available more readily than in the usual waking state. Erickson's emphasis on hypnosis with brevity was beneficial in times of war in dealing with soldiers emotionally traumatized by battle conditions (Erickson, 1939, 1967).

In response to the question posed at the beginning of this chapter, hypnosis, as we know it today, simply involves a heightened state of suggestibility. It involves neither magic nor mysticism. However, many scientists still are debating its basis and value and this will be discussed in subsequent chapters. As we shall see in the remainder of this book, theory and research in the study of hypnosis have come a long way, even since Erickson's important contributions. However, there is still a long way to go. Many innovative ideas helping to advance the scientific study of hypnosis and its applications are discussed in each of the remaining chapters. When you read about these advances, you should keep a historical perspective. In terms of our present knowledge of hypnosis, mesmerism is merely a

quaint relic of a bygone era. However, it should be remem-
bered that without the brave scientists who dared practice and
openly discuss altered states of consciousness at scientific
meetings, when such activities were akin to blasphemy,
research in hypnosis still would be at the level of animal
magnetism.

In terms of the modern applications of hypnosis, chapter 2
will focus on methods of assessing hypnotic susceptibility and
subsequent hypnotizability. These methods include the Harvard Group Scale of Hypnotic Susceptibility, the Stanford
Scale of Hypnotic Susceptibility, and the Barber Suggestibility
Scale. Personality, perception, and other correlates of hypnotic
susceptibility also will be discussed in this chapter. Furthermore, methods of enhancing hypnotic susceptibility for those
subjects normally deemed difficult to hypnotize will be
discussed.

The major concern of chapter 3 will be the beneficial
psychotherapeutic uses of hypnosis in various behavioral
disorders. Among the applications to be discussed will be the
use of hypnosis in the treatment of phobias, obsessions,
compulsions, and anxiety. Examples of how such disorders are
treated with hypnotherapy will be discussed using several case
studies from research. The chapter also will point out when
hypnotherapy is most or least beneficial.

Chapter 4 will be concerned primarily with applications
of hypnosis in the relief of pain. Examples from medical and
allied fields will be given—such fields as surgery, obstetrics,
and dentistry. The alternatives of hypnotic anesthesia and hypnotic analgesia in lieu of chemical means of reducing pain sensations will be stressed. In addition, the safety of hypnotic pain
reduction over chemical means of pain relief will be considered. For example, in anesthesia, hypnosis will be compared
with such anesthetics as sodium pentathol and novocaine. For
analgesia, hypnosis will be compared with such chemical analgesics as aspirin and Tylenol.

Sexual dysfunction and hypnosis will be the topic of discussion in chapter 5. Uses of hypnosis with such sexual dysfunctions as psychological frigidity and psychological
impotence will be discussed with adequate documentation

from published research. This treatment procedure will be compared with other treatment methods. Hypnosis as a potential means for enhancing sexual excitement and enjoyment during intercourse also will be discussed.

The aim of chapter 6 will be to examine the applied uses of hypnosis in the control of habits one wishes to reduce or eliminate. These include such common habits as smoking and overeating. Illustrations from published research will be cited to demonstrate how hypnosis can help control unwanted habits. Hypnotic techniques will be compared with other techniques for controlling or changing habits such as behavior modification and psychotherapy.

Chapter 7 will focus on the uses of hypnosis in restoring and enhancing memory of past experiences or events. Such documented phenomena as age regression, restoration of eidetic imagery (photographic memory) via hypnotic age regression, and the retention of information for longer than average periods of time with the aid of hypnosis will be discussed and illustrated from published research. In addition, the use of hypnosis in improving various perceptual and motor skills will be discussed and documented. These include the improvement of bowling accuracy and swimming ability.

The major topic in chapter 8 will be the comparisons of hypnosis to sleep and of the production of dreams during sleep and during hypnosis. This area of hypnosis research will be discussed in light of recent laboratory findings and documentation from published research. Also, the effects of hypnosis on ESP abilities will be discussed.

Chapter 9 will explain how the stage hypnotist performs his act. A detailed description of how this individual selects subjects, performs hypnosis before an audience, and entertains his audience with various demonstrations will be delineated. The primary focus of this chapter will be, then, to give away the trade secrets of the stage hypnotist and put his act into proper perspective. Furthermore, stage hypnosis, professional ethics, moral obligations, and the law will be discussed.

Predictions concerning the future of hypnosis in society will be the focus of chapter 10. Such issues as future and potential applications of hypnosis will be discussed. Furthermore, the ramifications of potential malpractice suits for those employing hypnosis as a professional treatment also will be mentioned.

In addition to the aforementioned chapters, a simple self-administered hypnotic susceptibility scale is included by which you, the reader, can determine in a relatively short period of time whether you are susceptible to hypnotic suggestions.

2

Hypnotizability

INDIVIDUALS SEEKING INFORMATION on hypnosis often ask, "Do you think that I can be hypnotized?" This question is not easy to answer without first requiring the individual to perform some type of task or tasks that indicate a willingness to cooperate with suggestions from a hypnotist. These tasks are often labeled under the general rubric, "hypnotic susceptibility tests."

Assessing Hypnotic Susceptibility

The most commonly employed tests or scales include the Stanford Hypnotic Susceptibility Scales (Weitzenhoffer and Hilgard, 1959, 1962), the Barber Suggestibility Scale (Barber and Glass, 1962), and the Harvard Group Scale of Hypnotic Susceptibility (Shor and Orne, 1962). Frequently, one or more of these standardized scales is employed by a hypnotist to determine the level of hypnotic responsiveness of an individual and the potential likelihood that the individual can be hypnotized. Descriptions of each of these scales will indicate exactly how a hypnotist can determine an individual's level of hypnotic susceptibility.

11

The Stanford scales were developed, as the name indicates, at Stanford University. Three forms of this scale were developed (Forms A, B, and C). However, traditionally, only one form is administered to a given participant. The scale is administered on an individual basis: that is, only one person takes the test at a given time. The hypnotic susceptibility testing session involves twelve parts or tasks. Each task consists of an action that the individual is asked by the administrator to perform. The tasks are arranged in a hierarchy of difficulty. Most individuals usually can comply with the first few suggestions. However, subsequent suggestions, especially the last few, usually can be followed by only a relatively small number of persons in the population. The more suggestions with which an individual complies, the greater is his hypnotic susceptibility level and the greater the ease with which he can be hypnotized. If an individual scores low on the scale, this does not preclude all chances of his being able to be hypnotized. However, it greatly reduces the chances. Methods for possibly improving an individual's susceptibility level will be considered later in this chapter.

The twelve tasks on one of the Stanford scales (Form A) are as follows. The first and easiest task is referred to as the *postural sway*. The subject is asked to close his eyes. The administrator then suggests to the subject that he is slowly falling backward (or forward). If he complies with this suggestion, he is considered to have performed the task adequately.

The second task on the Stanford scale is called *eye closure*. The participant, with his eyes open, is given the suggestion that his eyelids are becoming heavier and heavier. He is told that his eyelids are becoming so heavy and tired that he no longer can keep his eyes open. Compliance with this suggestion indicates successful performance of this task.

Hand lowering is the third task on the Stanford scale. The subject is asked to extend one of his arms in front of his body. Then the suggestion is given that his hand is becoming very heavy, so heavy that he can no longer keep his hand from falling. If the subject's hand falls approximately five to six inches from its original position, his performance in complying with this suggestion is considered adequate.

The fourth Stanford task is called *arm immobilization*. This task is basically the opposite of the third. Instead of the individual being told that his arm (hand) is falling, he is told that his extended arm is becoming so heavy that he cannot lift it from the original position. If he does not lift his arm or lifts it only slightly (not more than one inch), he is considered to have performed adequately on this task.

A fifth task on the Stanford scale is referred to as the *finger lock* procedure. The participant is requested to interlock the fingers of both hands. He is given a suggestion that he cannot separate his hands from one another. He is told that they have become one solid mass and are totally inseparable. Then he is asked to try as hard as he can to separate his hands. A slight separation of the hands, or none at all, is considered sufficient for passing this test.

Arm rigidity is the sixth Stanford task. As in two of the previous tasks, the individual is asked to extend his arm in front of his body. He is requested to make his arm as rigid as possible. Following this request, he is asked to try to bend his arm. An inability to bend the arm more than two inches is considered adequate performance for this task.

The next hypnotic susceptibility task on the Stanford scale requires *moving hands together*. First the individual is required to separate his hands by about twelve inches with the palms facing each other. Then he is asked to imagine that a magnetic force is attracting his hands, pulling them together. If this suggestion is followed and his hands are sufficiently close together (not more than six inches apart) after several seconds, this is considered adequate performance on this task item.

Verbal inhibition is the eighth task on the Stanford scale. The relaxed participant is given a suggestion that when he is asked to enunciate his name, he will have extreme difficulty in doing so. An inability to say one's name indicates passing performance for this task.

One of the more difficult tasks for subjects on the Stanford scale is the *fly hallucination* suggestion. The individual is given a suggestion that a fly is buzzing about his body and is becoming rather annoying. If he acknowledges the fly's presence by grabbing at it or performing some similar movement, he is considered to have complied adequately with the suggestion.

Eye catalepsy is the next task. While the subject's eyes are closed, he is told that his eyes will feel as if they have been glued shut. Then he is requested to try to open his eyes. A failure to open his eyes is taken as proof that eye catalepsy resulted from suggestion, and is rated as adequate performance.

The final two tasks or suggestions on the Stanford scale are considered the most difficult: the giving of a *posthypnotic suggestion* by the experimenter to the subject and the production of *hypnotic amnesia*. In the former suggestion, the subject is told that after the susceptibility testing session has been concluded, he will, for some unknown reason, want to change chairs upon hearing a tapping noise (or any signal that the administrator wishes to employ). If the individual does comply with the posthypnotic suggestion, he has performed adequately on this task.

An assessment of the presence of hypnotic amnesia requires the subject to recall the tasks which he previously was asked to perform. After being told that he will be unable to recall them, he is asked to enumerate aloud or in writing those tasks in which he does remember participating. The ability to recall no more than three tasks is taken as adequate performance on the amnesia test.

After all of the aforementioned tasks have been attempted by the individual whose hypnotic susceptibility level is being evaluated, the administrator determines, via the criteria previously mentioned, the number of tasks that were performed adequately. If a person complied with nine to twelve of the suggestions, he is considered to be highly susceptible to subsequent hypnotic suggestions. Compliance with the suggestions of three or fewer tasks is generally interpreted as indication that the individual is not readily hypnotizable. Compliance with the suggestions of four to eight instructional tasks is the level at which the average person performs. At this level it is very probable that a person can be hypnotized to follow many suggestions, but not as many as those scoring higher. It should be mentioned that the specific tasks an individual adequately completes are not important for establishing the level of hypnotic susceptibility. However, in general, the suggestions contained in the more difficult tasks are performed adequately by only highly susceptible individuals.

Another scale, which, like the Stanford scale, is administered on an individual basis, is the Barber Suggestibility Scale. This scale contains only eight tasks to be performed and scored. They include several which are quite similar to those found on the Stanford scale, namely *arm or hand lowering*, *hands-locked-in-lap*, and *verbal inhibition*. Five tasks, however, differ slightly or completely from the Stanford scale items. The first of these five is called *arm levitation*. In this task the individual is asked to extend one arm horizontally. Then the administrator suggests to the participant that his arm will begin to rise above its original position. If the arm rises four or more inches, this indicates adequate performance on the task.

The second of the differing Barber tasks is a *suggestion of extreme thirst*. There are two parts to this task. If the individual swallows or moistens his lips during the thirst suggestion, he is considered to have demonstrated half the requirement for sufficient performance. To show complete compliance, the individual also must indicate during a posthypnotic interview that, in fact, he was thirsty during the suggestion.

Another Barber task item is termed *body immobility*. A seated participant is given the suggestion that he will be unable to stand. If he does not stand at all within fifteen seconds after being given a command to stand, he is considered to have exhibited adequate performance. If he stands after five seconds but before fifteen seconds, he receives half credit. This scoring procedure is also used in the hands-locked-in-lap task as well as the verbal inhibition task.

Posthypnotic responsiveness is a fourth differing task on the Barber scale. This one is comparable to the Stanford scale's posthypnotic task of moving to a different chair, except that on the Barber scale the posthypnotic response is to cough to a click initiated by the test administrator. If the individual coughs, he has adequately demonstrated compliance with the suggestion of this task.

A final task on the Barber scale is the production of
selective amnesia. This task is similar to the amnesic task on
the Stanford scale. However, on the Barber scale the subject is
asked to remember all the tasks in which he performed except
the arm levitation task (until given a cue to remember this task
also). If he performs as instructed, he has adequately demonstrated selective amnesia.

If a participant receives six to eight points on the Barber
scale, one point for each task adequately completed and one-
half point for partial completions as previously delineated, he
is considered highly susceptible to hypnosis instructions. The
average performance on the Barber scale is around 4.5 points
(Barber and Calverley, 1963).

The third commonly administered and standardized hypnosis scale was developed at Harvard University and is appro-
priately referred to as the Harvard Group Scale of Hypnotic
Susceptibility. Unlike the previously mentioned scales, this
scale is administered in a group setting. In addition, the individuals being evaluated are permitted to score their own levels
of hypnotic susceptibility. This scale has one distinct advantage over the Stanford and Barber scales: many individuals can
be evaluated simultaneously. However, because more distractions occur in a group testing situation than in individual testing sessions, this may, in some instances, be counterproduc-
tive. Also, there exists the potential for inaccurate evaluations
of hypnotic susceptibility levels. Fortunately, fear of this
potential disadvantage has been dispelled (Bentler and Hilgard, 1963). It has been determined that .74 is the correlation
between individual- and group-assessed hypnotic susceptibility levels. Thus, in general, scores on all the scales are fairly
comparable.

The Harvard scale, like the Stanford scale, consists of
twelve tasks to be performed, nine of which are exactly the
same as those on the Stanford scale. The other three tasks on
the Harvard scale—*head falling, communication inhibition,*
and *posthypnotic suggestion*—are similar to Stanford scale
tasks.

Head falling is comparable to the postural sway task on
the Stanford scale, not only in terms of degree of difficulty, but
also in terms of the act itself. Instead of suggesting that the in-

dividual's body will fall backward or forward, this Harvard scale task item suggests that his head will fall forward. If it does fall forward about two inches, this is taken as adequate performance in following the suggestion.

Communication inhibition is comparable to the verbal inhibition task on the Stanford scale. Instead of the individual being told that he will be unable to enunciate his name, this Harvard scale task suggests that he will be unable to shake his head to indicate "no." If the participant cannot shake his head as indicated when asked to do so, this is considered adequate performance on this task.

The task referred to as *posthypnotic suggestion* is practically identical to the task of the same name on the Stanford scale. However, instead of being given the posthypnotic suggestion of changing chairs upon the presentation of some precipitating stimulus, the participant is given the posthypnotic suggestion of touching his ankle.

It is apparent from the descriptions of each of the most commonly employed standardized evaluative tools for assessing hypnotic susceptibility that it is rather time-consuming to determine the extent or level of hypnotizability of an individual. As a result, investigators have attempted to develop rapid screening procedures whereby a single task could be used to determine in a few minutes whether an individual can readily be hypnotized. One might ask, "Why is it necessary to have an individual attempt to perform all eight tasks of the Barber scale or all twelve tasks of the Harvard or Stanford scales?" The answer is that it is not necessary if one simply wishes to ascertain whether that individual can readily be hypnotized. The primary reason for asking participants to perform on many tasks is to determine exact and specific levels of hypnotizability for use in scientific investigations. Investigators in the field of hypnosis most often prefer specific types of subjects to serve under different conditions. A common dichotomization is the comparison of high- and low-susceptibility subjects. In order to form these subject categories, it is necessary to have subjects perform preexperimentally on many screening tasks.

If a person simply wishes to know if he can be hypnotized, could he participate in only one or two of the tasks of the aforementioned tests? If so, which ones? The answer to the first question is "yes." In determining which tasks to ask the person to perform, it is probably best to start with one of the easier suggestions (e.g., postural sway or eye closure). The reason for this is that very few individuals are capable of performing adequately on the more difficult items (e.g., fly hallucination or amnesia), yet most individuals can be hypnotized! Therefore, a fast screening procedure such as the postural sway or the hand clasp (finger lock) usually will indicate to the hypnotist which individuals can be hypnotized. This procedure often is used by the stage hypnotist to select subjects from his audience for his later demonstrations. Those individuals who follow his suggestions best and most readily become his "volunteers." This and other aspects of stage hypnotism will be discussed in greater detail in chapter 9.

In addition to the use of individual task items from standardized tests to rapidly assess hypnotic susceptibility, several other procedures have been employed. One of them is referred to as the eye-roll test (Spiegel, 1970). In this test the subject is requested to open his eyes wide and to roll his eyeballs upward. Then he is requested to lower his eyelids without rolling the eyeballs down. Those capable of performing this procedure were found to be easily hypnotizable. However, the correlation between performance on the eye-roll test and hypnotic susceptibility scores on standardized scales generally was found to be weak (Wheeler, et al., 1974). Therefore, although the eye-roll test may be predictive of hypnotic susceptibility for some individuals, it is not a universal predictor.

Another factor which appears to be more strongly related to hypnotic susceptibility is an individual's level of creativity. Perry, Wilder, and Appignanesi (1973) found that persons judged to be highly creative on a battery of tests used to assess this attribute also were found to be highly susceptible to hypnosis. This relationship was found to be strongest for female participants.

Other variables also have been found to correlate highly with the level of hypnotic susceptibility. Wallace and Garrett (1973) and Wallace, Garrett, and Anstadt (1974) found that when individuals were asked to observe a small, stationary spot of light in an otherwise dark environment, they perceived the light as moving. This visual illusion is referred to as the autokinetic effect. Wallace and his collaborators found that subjects prejudged to be highly susceptible to hypnosis reported a greater frequency (more direction changes) of movement than low-susceptibility individuals. Miller (1975) and Wallace, Knight, and Garrett (1976) also found a strong relationship between the level of hypnotic susceptibility and the perception of other types of visual illusions. Although this is interesting, these correlates of hypnotic susceptibility are not more efficient than subtasks from standardized hypnosis scales as general screening tests of hypnotic susceptibility. Both types are time-consuming to administer and to evaluate. In addition, the standardized subtasks have been shown, for the most part, to be valid predictors of hypnotic susceptibility. This is not always the case for the aforementioned correlates of hypnotic susceptibility.

Why are some persons more susceptible to hypnosis than others and why do they respond better to hypnotic suggestions? This is a difficult question to answer. Many investigators have sought and are continuing to seek an answer or, at least, a partial answer to this question. Some factors which have been considered are the ability of an individual to have positive attitudes concerning the acceptance of a suggestion from a hypnotist, to be motivated to perform when a suggestion is given, and to have positive expectancies of the test situation (Barber, Spanos, and Chaves, 1974). An individual who anticipates that he can be hypnotized, who has positive attitudes toward hypnosis, and who is motivated to accept suggestions probably will be fairly easy to hypnotize. On the other hand, an individual who does not believe in hypnosis and who is not sufficiently motivated to try to be hypnotized probably will be very difficult to hypnotize.

Modifying Susceptibility

What about the person who is motivated and who wants to be hypnotized but who fails to adequately follow the suggestions of a hypnotist no matter how hard he tries? Since there are individuals in this category, it would appear that there must be other factors that reduce hypnotic susceptibility. If this is the case, it should be possible, perhaps through various techniques and training procedures, to help an individual enhance his hypnotic susceptibility level. Although at one time hypnotic susceptibility level was believed to be a nonmodifiable or stable trait (Hilgard, 1965), no longer is it believed to be. In fact, several techniques for modifying hypnotic susceptibility have been tried with some success (Diamond, 1974). These methods include: (a) modifying susceptibility by means of sensory alterations, (b) modifying susceptibility by varying the subject's set of mind, or expectancies, (c) modifying susceptibility through nonhypnotic training experiences, and (d) modifying susceptibility through training in hypnotic and hypnotic-like behavior.

In attempts to modify susceptibility with the assistance of sensory alterations, several methods have been employed. Borlone, Dittborn, and Palestrini (1962) found that suggestion-induced sleep can be converted to hypnosis with appropriate instructions. If one were to generalize beyond this finding, it could be stated that an individual normally difficult to hypnotize might well be hypnotizable if hypnotic suggestions were to be given while he was approaching a state of sleep.

Others have found that white noise (such as one might hear on an improperly tuned radio station) and monotony enhance hypnotic susceptibility and subsequent hypnotic performance (Oswald, 1959; Williams, 1952). Also, such psychedelic drugs as LSD-25 and mescaline have been found to increase hypnotic susceptibility and subsequent responsiveness to hypnotic suggestions (Ulett, Akpinar, and Itil, 1972; Sjoberg and Hollister, 1965).

Sensory restriction and isolation also tend to increase hypnotic performance. When individuals have been isolated from sounds and visual experiences for periods as short as thirty minutes (Wickramasekera, 1969) or as long as three to six hours (Pena, 1963; Sanders and Reyher, 1969), hypnotic susceptibility has been found to increase in subjects normally deemed difficult to hypnotize.

Several investigators have found that a change in the level of hypnotic susceptibility can result from changes in various aspects of the subject's set of mind concerning hypnosis, or expectancies of hypnosis, or the conditions for hypnotic induction. For example, Barber and Calverley (1964) and Wickramasekera (1971) found that when individuals are told that they will be hypnotized, as opposed to labeling the situation in some other way, they are easier to hypnotize. Barber and Calverley (1965) have found that repeated suggestions of relaxation, drowsiness, and sleep also are effective in increasing responsiveness to hypnotic task suggestions.

Motivating instructions, given when administering hypnotic task suggestions, also have been found to increase hypnotic responsiveness (Barber, 1969). For example, if the suggestion to the participant includes instructions designed to increase his motivation to adhere to the suggestion, it has been reported that the individual responds more readily to that suggestion. In addition, if his attitudes are such that he believes he will be hypnotized, it is likely he will be (Diamond, 1970; Gregory and Diamond, 1973; Shor, 1971).

If an individual's expectancies are changed, could his hypnotic susceptibility be increased? In other words, can subjects of low- or moderate-susceptibility be "made" more hypnotizable by changing their attitudes or beliefs concerning hypnosis and their ability to be hypnotized? The answer appears to be "yes" (Wilson, 1967; Gregory and Diamond, 1973). This was accomplished in the Gregory and Diamond study by administering a bogus personality test to individuals who subsequently were led to believe that they were hypnotizable as a result of their scores on the test.

Hypnotic susceptibility also can be increased if the person being tested or hypnotized has had some previous extended relationship with the hypnotist (Kramer, 1969) and has come to trust him well enough to follow his suggestions (Shor and Schatz, 1960; Tart, 1967). Therefore, if the participant is placed in a congenial setting that evokes confidence, the chances are greater that he can be hypnotized.

In addition, it has been found that certain nonhypnotic training procedures can be employed to increase a person's susceptibility to hypnotic suggestion. For example, training individuals to have more vivid imagery in a nonhypnotic setting has been found to increase subsequent susceptibility and responsiveness to hypnotic suggestions (Sutcliffe, Perry, and Sheehan, 1970). Also, training individuals to alter via biofeedback certain psychophysiological responses such as alpha brain waves (Engstrom, London, and Hart, 1970) or muscle responses (Wickramasekera, 1971, 1973) has been shown to increase hypnotic susceptibility. Furthermore, interpersonal-oriented encounter group training increases susceptibility (Shapiro and Diamond, 1972). In summary, it appears that the successful training of participants to be more relaxed, trusting, and attentive in the performance of the aforementioned non-hypnotic tasks, carries over to a hypnosis situation and increases an individual's hypnotic susceptibility level.

Hypnotic susceptibility also has been shown to be modifiable through training in hypnotic behavior. Zimbardo, Rapaport, and Baron (1969) reported beneficial effects from having individuals first observe a model behaving in a responsive fashion to hypnotic suggestions. Removing misconceptions about hypnosis by reading to the individual information directed toward this issue also has been found to increase hypnotic susceptibility (Cronin, Spanos, and Barber, 1971).

In conclusion, it has been shown by many investigators in the field of hypnosis that numerous methods can be used to temporarily increase an individual's susceptibility to hypnotic suggestion. Therefore, even if a person has scored low on one of the previously discussed hypnotic scales, he still may be able to be hypnotized with the use of prehypnotic training. This would mean that all individuals probably are capable of being hypnotized under some circumstances.

3

Hypnotherapy

BEHAVIORAL DISORDERS SUCH as phobias, obsessions, compulsions, and "free-floating" anxiety have been treated successfully with various types of behavior therapy, especially behavior modification techniques. Can hypnosis also be used by itself or in conjunction with other therapies to treat these disorders in a beneficial manner? How does the method employed by hypnosis to treat various disorders compare with traditional approaches? These are some of the questions that will be answered in this chapter.

Before hypnotherapy can be used beneficially for the treatment of any type of behavioral disorder, it is necessary, of course, to determine if the subject can easily be hypnotized. This is accomplished via the tests and techniques described in chapter 2. Naturally, if a subject cannot readily be hypnotized, hypnotherapy may not be the treatment of choice for his specific disorder. Although the individual can be taught to develop a greater susceptibility to hypnosis through some of the procedures described in chapter 2, this process may be somewhat time-consuming and, in the long run, other approaches to the treatment of his problem may be advisable.

If the subject is found to be readily hypnotizable, then it is desirable to establish a case history of his problem. For instance, if a spider phobia is to be treated, it is helpful to trace the development of the problem to its origin, if possible, since the phobia can be treated most effectively if its origin is known. If this cannot be accomplished, however, the phobia still can be treated in an effective manner.

Once hypnotizability and a case history have been established, treatment of the problem can commence. The problem areas that have been treated most beneficially with the use of hypnosis are those that were mentioned at the beginning of this chapter—phobic behavior, obsessive-compulsive behavior, and anxiety. Each of these behavioral disorders with concomitant hypnotic treatment will be described and comparisons will be made with treatment using nonhypnotic techniques.

Phobias

What is a phobia? This often used term is defined as an irrational fear. If an individual is fearful of animate or inanimate objects that, in and of themselves, are not harmful or capable of producing harm, this fear response may be labeled a phobia. Phobias may be manifested in various ways. For instance, responses to a phobia may include manifestations of anxiety such as screaming, crying, freezing up, escaping, or isolating oneself. In treating a phobia, one can deal with the response and/or the cause of the response. Treating only the response may produce alleviation of the phobia; however, for the most part, this will be only temporary. To achieve permanent removal of the phobia, it is necessary to discover the causes of the irrational fear. Thus, as was previously mentioned, the most effective treatment of a phobia is based on a detailed case history of the problem. Then, not only the response to the fear can be treated, but also the source of the fear itself.

A traditional method that has proved successful in the treatment of phobias is called desensitization. This term was coined by Lang and Lazovik (1963) in a study concerned with treatment of the fear of nonpoisonous snakes. Because fear of such creatures is basically irrational, as these snakes cannot cause any harm, this fear is called a snake phobia. The subjects employed by Lang and Lazovik reported that they habitually avoided going anywhere near a live snake, refused to enter the reptile section of a zoo, were afraid to walk through an open field, became upset and felt uneasy at seeing snakes in the movies or on television, and were even distressed at observing pictures of snakes in magazines.

After it was established that, in fact, the subjects did exhibit a fear of nonpoisonous snakes, each subject was individually tested to determine the extent of his phobia: namely, how fearful of snakes was the subject? This was determined by having each subject enter a room in which a five-foot-long black snake was housed in a glass case. The subject was requested to walk to the housing with the experimenter. When they arrived at this point, the experimenter removed a wire grill covering the top of the glass case and assured the subject that the snake was harmless. Then the subject was requested to come closer to the glass case, look down at the snake, and touch it. Following this sequence of events, the subject was asked to rate his fear on a ten-point scale in which ten was considered most fearful.

Once a fear level was established for the subject, the desensitization process was begun. Before actual treatment, a series of twenty situations involving snakes was described (e.g., writing the word "snake," accidentally stepping on a dead snake) and the subject was asked to grade each from most to least frightening. The subject then was required to undergo muscle relaxation therapy and to practice such relaxation at home every day for ten to fifteen minutes.

Actual desensitization therapy commenced after the subject had practiced his home relaxation exercises. First the subject was hypnotized and instructed to relax. Then he was asked to imagine the situation involving a snake which he previously had rated as least aversive or least anxiety-provoking. If the subject was able to remain relaxed during this imagination period, he was asked to imagine the next most distressing situation. This process continued until relaxation was achieved on each level of snake-associated fear. With the use of this method, the snake phobia was considerably reduced and subjects became capable of approaching and touching the snake which they had previously shunned and feared.

Since Lang and Lazovik treated only the fear response and not the cause of the snake phobia, one must ask if the phobia reappeared some months after desensitization therapy. After six months Lang and Lazovik found that the therapy was still in effect. Thus, desensitization teamed with hypnotic relaxation and imagination appears to be a potent therapy in the reduction and/or elimination of such phobias.

Because desensitization played such an important role in the success of the treatment, one wonders whether this success could have been achieved with the use of desensitization alone—without hypnosis. This would be an important concept for use with subjects who are not readily hypnotizable.

In the use of desensitization without hypnosis, it is desirable to employ gradations of real situations during the desensitization process. Instead of the subject being asked to imagine aversive situations, he is required to experience the situations. If this is not possible, the subject still may use imagery in a fashion similar to that employed with hypnosis, but it must be noted that the imagery, in all likelihood, will not be as vivid as with hypnosis. In addition, desensitization without the benefits of hypnotic imagery is more time-consuming. However, the end result is as impressive as it is when hypnosis is used in conjunction with desensitization. This is illustrated in a study by Paul (1966) in which the concern was with the treatment of anxiety associated with speaking before a group.

Paul compared systematic desensitization without hypnosis with insight-oriented psychotherapy as treatments for public speaking anxiety. In the former treatment, the therapist attempted to teach relaxation techniques along with gradual, systematic desensitization to situations in which anxiety had been associated with giving a speech. The latter technique involved attempts by the therapist to reduce public speaking anxiety by helping the patient gain insight into the bases and interrelationships of his problem. Results of this study clearly demonstrated that systematic desensitization was superior to insight-oriented psychotherapy: namely, with use of the former treatment, anxiety was most clearly reduced. Thus, desensitization with or without the use of hypnosis appears to be a potent means of dealing with phobias and associated anxieties.

Can hypnosis without desensitization also reduce anxiety associated with phobias? It can, but only temporarily. To cause the phobia and associated anxiety to dissipate to a considerable extent, it is necessary to develop a hierarchy of events from least to most anxiety-provoking in terms of the phobia, as did Lang and Lazovik, and to determine the degree of phobic reaction. Once this has been achieved, a systematic elimination of the phobia can take place through the learning of relaxation techniques. Without this systematic desensitization, successful results would be short-lived at best.

Thus, the most potent form of therapy to use in dealing with a phobic reaction is systematic desensitization in conjunction with relaxation and vivid imagery of phobic-associated events enhanced by means of hypnosis. This may be the case because the use of hypnosis appears to mediate therapeutic changes (Spanos, DeMoor, and Barber, 1973; Lazarus, 1963) since subjects who enter therapy usually believe hypnosis will facilitate their progress and, in fact, it usually does.

The systematic desensitization of a phobia using the method employed by Lang and Lazovik did not require the establishment of a case history of the phobia. However, as was mentioned earlier, a more lasting cure for the anxiety associated with a given phobia might be possible if the roots of the phobia were known. Several studies which have traced the history of individual phobias include those by Scott (1970) and Rothman, Carroll and Rothman (1976).

Scott was concerned with treating a young female for a severe phobia for birds. On first seeking treatment for the phobia, the patient had no memory of the cause of her irrational fear of birds. In addition, the patient also mentioned that she had extended her fear to other flying things, such as flies and moths. As this individual was readily hypnotizable, she was placed in a deep trance and age-regressed (taken back to an earlier period of her life with the aid of hypnosis). While in this state, she revealed that her grandfather had kept a few hens in his backyard when the patient was rather young (around five years of age). At this time in her life a white hen flew up to her and forced her against a wall. Subsequently, learning of this event, her uncle killed the hen and hung it in a cupboard. Later that day her grandfather gave her some money to put in a gas meter that was situated in the same cupboard. When she opened the cupboard, she became extremely frightened. This experience was the only memory she had of fear connected with birds and it was obtainable only with hypnotic age regression.

The therapist was able to use this information to develop a hierarchy of events from least to most anxiety-provoking with regard to the fear of birds and other flying, animate objects. Proceeding in a manner similar to that developed by Lang and Lazovik, Scott used systematic desensitization, and as a result of determining the possible cause of the phobia, was able to incorporate into the hierarchy those incidents from the patient's life that related to its development. This extension beyond the desensitization procedure of Lang and Lazovik theoretically should have produced a permanent extinction of the phobia. In fact, a follow-up on the patient one year after cessation of therapy showed that the phobia had disappeared.

In another study, Rothman, Carroll and Rothman (1976), a woman who feared going anywhere alone was treated in a manner similar to Scott's female patient. With the use of hypnosis, the possible source of her phobia was established. Then a hierarchy was developed incorporating events from her phobic developmental process. Ultimately, with the use of desensitization, her phobia was extinguished.

It appears then that the most potent treatment for a phobia is the combined use of systematic desensitization with hypnosis. The element of hypnosis is extremely important in: (a) reducing general anxiety to enable the patient to relax, (b) age-regressing the patient to that time in life when the phobia may have developed, and (c) helping the patient produce vivid imagery of events in the desensitization process. Again, it should be stated that patients not readily hypnotizable also can profit by systematic desensitization of a phobia. However, when hypnosis is possible for a given patient, the extinction of the phobia is far quicker and probably more permanent (Scott, 1970).

Obsessions and Compulsions

Both behavior modification techniques and hypnosis have been employed in the treatment of obsessions and compulsions. An obsession is a persistent idea, image, or desire that dominates one's thoughts or feelings. A compulsion is a strong, usually irresistible impulse to perform an act that is contrary to the voluntary will of the individual. Generally, both these disorders are treated in a similar manner or as one disorder under the rubric, obsessive-compulsive behavior. An individual categorized as an obsessive-compulsive is, in every sense of the word, a perfectionist. As described by Dengrove (1976), he is extremely neat, systematic, conscientious, orderly, concerned that everything should be in its right place, and certain that there is a right place for everything. As a result, this individual can never achieve absolute perfection and, therefore, has feelings of inadequacy with accompanying anxiety.

As with phobias, several types of treatments are available to deal with irrational obsessions (e.g., terrible thoughts of doing physical harm to someone you love) and compulsions (e.g., washing your hands ten times each hour). If hypnosis is to be used in treatment, first it is necessary, as in the treatment of any disorder, to determine if a given patient can easily be hypnotized. Second, if possible, the genesis of the behavioral disorder should be determined. Once this information is procured, therapy can commence.

Therapy for obsessive-compulsive behavior tends to follow three basic strategies (Coleman, 1976): (a) helping the individual to discriminate between thought and action, to accept his thoughts and ideas as common to most people, and to integrate them into his self-structure; (b) helping the individual to discriminate between objective and imagined dangers and to respond selectively to each; and (c) blocking obsessive-compulsive rituals by consistently rewarding the person when he departs from or abandons the use of such irrational behavior.

These strategies were recognized early, and Donley (1908) incorporated hypnosis in the treatment of a young man who was obsessed with the thought that a comet was going to strike Earth and destroy it. It was learned that this obsession first developed when the patient read a newspaper article about a comet approaching the vicinity of Earth. Treatment included confirmation of the genesis of the obsession with age regression through hypnosis. Upon confirmation of the origin of the problem, the patient was given suggestions under hypnosis that his anxiety associated with his obsession and the obsession itself had its origin in the newspaper article and that his belief had no basis in fact. He accepted this suggestion and in a matter of a few weeks reported that he was no longer troubled with the comet obsession. In fact, he acknowledged that he now knew the newspaper article was misleading and there was no reasonable basis for his previous belief.

It should be mentioned that Donley's patient was judged to be extremely intelligent. Therefore, it is not surprising that treatment with hypnosis was both swift and extremely effective. In fact, it is very likely that the patient simply used logic with the aid of hypnotic suggestions to help rid himself of his obsession. The relatively brief period of time involved in freeing the patient of this obsession is probably not representative of obsession elimination time in the average patient. However, this example does illustrate the usefulness of hypnosis in the treatment of obsessive behavior.

Compulsions also have been treated successfully with hypnosis. Brenman and Knight (1945) report the case of a young girl with compulsive hopping behavior. Although this patient had many behavioral disorders, she particularly exhibited a severe case of hopping for no apparent or rational reason. This behavior usually commenced with the patient running, instead of walking, to a point of destination and concluded with compulsive hopping on her right leg for hours at a time in a violent manner. At first the patient was resistant to any therapy, but finally agreed to cooperate if she would be permitted to hop for a certain period each day. With this bargain in mind, the patient was hypnotized and it was suggested to her that her general tension and restlessness would decrease so that she would not need to hop so violently. Subsequently, when the patient was allowed to hop during the agreed-upon period, she found herself unable to do so. She continued to try but without success. This simple suggestion given under hypnosis for two successive days was sufficient to eliminate a hopping compulsion which had not been treated successfully with more traditional psychotherapeutic methods (Brenman and Knight, 1945).

This example should not suggest that all compulsive behavior can be extinguished so easily and quickly. On the contrary, it usually takes much longer just to compile a history on the development of the compulsion. However, since Brenman and Knight were not the first therapists to see the patient, the historical development of the problem was, at least, partially known. Most compulsive behavior requires a lengthier treatment period than the one in the hopping example. This time factor, however, is considerably reduced if a patient can be hypnotized to permit the introduction of hypnotic suggestions during therapy.

Kroger (1976) presents a therapy combining hypnosis and behavior modification which he reports has been successful with compulsions as well as disorders such as phobias, obesity and smoking (see chapter 6). Basically, his therapy consists of several stages. The first stage involves determining the historical development of the problem and providing a professional diagnosis. In the second stage, hypnosis is introduced. This is to determine an individual's level of hypnotic susceptibility and to produce relaxation for the patient's body. During hypnosis Kroger employs behavior modification techniques of rewarding appropriate behavior (e.g., not exhibiting the compulsive behavior being treated). In this manner the patient develops an association between pleasant feelings from relaxation suggestions produced through hypnosis and not behaving in a compulsive fashion. When compulsive behavior does occur, the pleasant and relaxed feeling is absent; therefore, the patient learns that only noncompulsive behavior is rewarding (i.e., pleasant and nonanxiety-provoking). In addition, the patient is taught self-hypnosis so that he can administer his own pleasant, relaxation reward when appropriate. In this manner compulsive behavior is usually extinguished.

In combining behavior modification techniques with hypnosis after determining possible causes for a given disorder, such as a compulsion, Kroger and others (Cautela, 1975; Platonov, 1955; Paterson, 1967) have found such an approach to produce results more durable and less likely to extinguish than the sole use of any other psychotherapeutic approach including behavior modification.

"Free-Floating" Anxiety

Another common behavior disorder that has been treated successfully with hypnosis is "free-floating" anxiety. This type of anxiety is not the same as that experienced by individuals with phobias or obsessive-compulsive behavior. In their case a reason for the anxiety generally is known and, thus, can be labeled. Free-floating anxiety, on the other hand, often is not attached to any particular event or phenomenon, yet produces acute attacks of uneasiness. According to Wolpe (1969), this indicates that the source or eliciting stimulus of the anxiety is obscure, complex, and quite pervasive. Some of the behavior resulting from such anxiety includes inability to concentrate, difficulty in making decisions, extreme sensitivity, discouragement, sleep disturbances, excessive sweating, and sustained muscle tension (Coleman, 1976).

Coleman also enumerates four general reasons why free-floating anxiety might occur. The first is conditioning or learning to be anxious because those around you are in this state. Thus, a child may learn from his parents to be anxious because he models their behavior.

A second source of anxiety development stems from the inability to handle "dangerous" impulses such as hostility or resentment. Anxiety may be experienced as a result of situations that elicit these feelings—that is, feelings that might devalue the individual's self-image or endanger his relationships with other people. Instead of coping with the situation in an assertive manner, the individual acts with compliance and subservience. The end result is that the patient experiences free-floating anxiety.

Another source enumerated by Coleman is a situation in which making a decision may be anxiety-provoking. Faced with a decision which may involve conflicts over moral values or possible loss of security and status, the individual may develop acute attacks of anxiety.

A final reason given by Coleman for the production of anxiety attacks is the reactivation of prior trauma. For example, anxiety may be produced in a work situation if an employee has developed an unconscious association between criticisms lodged against him by his present foreman and criticisms he received as a child from his father. When he was criticized by his father, anxiety was produced. As a result, anxiety is produced again when criticisms emanate from his foreman.

Given the aforementioned reasons by Coleman for the production of anxiety, it should be emphasized once again that the patient usually is not aware of the genesis of his anxiety. This has been ascertained in interviews with the patient. Thus, it is labeled "free-floating" anxiety.

Psychotherapy has been used to treat this behavioral disorder (Coleman, 1976) by helping the patient discriminate between real and imagined dangers, by teaching the patient more effective methods of coping, and by modifying conditions in his life situation that are serving to maintain his maladaptive behavior. If behavior modification techniques are employed in the treatment of free-floating anxiety, the therapist first would try to discover the environmental conditions that are reinforcing and maintaining the maladaptive behavior. This information could be obtained by an in-depth interview of the patient. However, it will be recalled that, more often than not, the patient does not know why he feels anxious. Therefore, determination of precipitating reasons for experienced anxiety would require more than an interview. It could require observing the individual in his habitat for a period of time and noting when anxiety attacks are produced. This would be rather time-consuming, however, and might not even be profitable. There is no assurance that anxiety-provoking events would be discovered during the observation period and recognized as the cause of the patient's uneasiness. In addition, even if they were discovered, one still would have to determine the genesis of the anxiety to provide a long-lasting alleviation of the maladaptive state.

A possible solution to the inadequacies of the sole use of behavior modification in the treatment of maladaptive anxiety is a reliance on hypnosis as a part of the treatment. As with the treatment of phobias and obsessive-compulsive behavior, the dual use of hypnosis with behavior modification may prove to be the most potent form of treatment.

Employing hypnosis in the treatment of anxiety, Lazarus (1963) has reported that if a patient is asked to simulate a state of sensory deprivation during hypnosis and is reinforced for this behavior by the relaxation and calmness he experiences, a marked reduction in free-floating anxiety results. Sensory deprivation may be induced in many different ways. In the strictest sense such deprivation involves the elimination of visual, auditory, tactual (touch), olfactory (smell), and gustatory (taste) sources of information for a period of time. Rarely, however, are all five senses restricted.

Simulated deprivation involves the gradual reduction or elimination of sensory information with the aid of hypnotic suggestions. For example, a subject may be told under hypnosis that he is losing all sense of touch. This might approximate a type of induced hypnotic anesthesia (see chapter 4). He also may be given suggestions of the reduction of auditory and visual information so that there is less such information impinging upon his system. When such states are induced under hypnosis, a feeling of anxiety often is replaced with a state of calmness. However, for this type of therapy to be most successful in the treatment of anxiety, it is advantageous to teach the patient self-hypnosis. If this is accomplished, the patient can induce his own state of relaxation and calmness, thereby reducing the necessity for visiting the therapist whenever an attack of anxiety occurs. A complete elimination of anxiety attacks may not be possible for most individuals afflicted with this behavioral disorder, as it often is difficult to determine the exact cause of a long-standing anxiety. Thus, more often than not, the symptom is treated rather than the cause. This produces relief from anxiety attacks but not its total elimination. Currently, no bona fide psychotherapeutic treatment is available that has been shown capable of totally eliminating all occurrences of free-floating anxiety from an afflicted patient.

In summary, as is evident from the described therapies for treating phobias, obsessions, compulsions, and free-floating anxiety, the most potent form of treatment involves the combined use of hypnosis and behavior modification techniques. Behavior modification is a potent form of treatment in its own right. However, hypnosis expedites its therapeutic effects and this results in relief for the patient from the anxiety-provoking maladaptive behaviors described in this chapter.

4

Hypnotic Anesthesia and Analgesia

ONE OF THE most provocative uses of hypnosis in today's society is its application in the relief of pain. Hypnosis as a general anesthetic has been used most often in medical surgery, obstetrics, and dentistry. Hypnotic anesthesia involves the attempt to prevent pain from occurring. Hypnotic analgesia is concerned with the removal of existing pain.

Hypnosis and Surgery

It may surprise the reader to learn that hypnosis was used in medical surgery as an anesthetic before chemical anesthetics were discovered. However, as with the use of hypnosis in general, its use in medicine was not well accepted. Only a few surgeons like Esdaile (1850) dared to employ this procedure (see chapter 1). His use of hypnosis as an anesthetic was not necessarily a rebellious act against the medical profession or society. It represented the only known means of reducing pain before and during surgery. As a result of the absence of any known chemical agent which would reduce surgical pain, patients often refused to be operated on, some choosing even death over the anticipated, excruciating pain. Even with non-anesthetic surgery, the mortality rate was quite high (forty percent). Frequently, death resulted not from surgical error, but from the experienced pain and the inability of the patient to remain sufficiently still and calm for the surgeon to perform his dangerous task. However, with the use of hypnotic anesthesia which allowed the patient to remain more calm and relaxed, Esdaile reported a comparably low mortality rate (five percent).

With the advent of chemical anesthetics, such as chloroform, ether, and sodium thiopental (Pentothal), hypnotic anesthesia almost disappeared from use. Although chemical anesthetics have been extremely effective in reducing or eliminating surgical pain, all such drugs have many dangerous side effects, the most important and serious of which is respiratory depression or the inability to breath in a normal manner while under the influence of the drug. Other side effects include myocardial depression, cardiac arrhythmias, prolonged laryngospasm, and shivering. In some instances, death has resulted from the administration of a chemical anesthetic, usually because of complications with breathing. As a result of adverse drug effects, many surgeons have reintroduced the use of hypnotic anesthesia before and during surgery for the relief of pain. As this type of anesthetic is free of all the side effects inherent in the use of chemical anesthetics, some persons were led to believe that hypnotic anesthesia could be a complete substitute for the drugs.

However, not all individuals can readily be hypnotized, let alone hypnotically anesthesized (see chapter 2). As a matter of fact, hypnotic anesthesia has been estimated to be effective in about only ten percent of all patients who undergo surgery (Kroger, 1963). Therefore, some surgeons began employing a combination of chemical and hypnotic anesthetics for those patients who showed some initial susceptibility to hypnotic suggestion.

One may ask at this point, why use hypnotic anesthesia at all if a chemical agent still is necessary for the relief of pain? Surgeons who employ hypnotic anesthesia do so because it enables them to use a less concentrated dose of a chemical agent. In other words, there is a positive trade-off when hypnotic anesthesia is employed: the more effective hypnotic anesthesia is in the relief of pain, the less of the chemical anesthetic necessary. With reduced dosage, the possibility of producing undesirable side effects is considerably reduced. Therefore, the dual use of chemical and hypnotic anesthesia allows for a less risky surgical procedure.

Despite the advantage of this reduced surgical risk, many surgeons familiar with hypnotic anesthesia procedures fail to use them because of the lengthy advance process they require; it is far easier and less time-consuming to administer a drug. Those surgeons who are sufficiently patient to employ hypnotic anesthesia spend many sessions with their patients before the actual surgical procedure.

What procedures are employed by the surgeon to ensure effective hypnotic anesthesia or the elimination of pain? Prior to the use of hypnotic anesthesia in surgery, it is necessary, of course, to determine if the patient can be hypnotized. This can be ascertained in a relatively short period of time by employing some of the tests for assessing hypnotic susceptibility delineated in chapter 2. Naturally, most surgeons do not administer a complete hypnotic susceptibility scale to a patient because of the time it requires. Instead, they may select certain items from one of the scales, such as arm rigidity or the hand clasp. Generally, a patient who is capable of following these types of suggestions also is capable of receiving hypnotic anesthesia suggestions. In addition, Hilgard and Hilgard (1975) and Wallace (1976) have found evidence that the more susceptible the subject is to hypnosis, the stronger will be the suggestion, or in the case of surgery, the stronger the effect of hypnotic anesthesia. As a result, although it is time-consuming, a surgeon may be doing his patient and himself a disservice by not determining the patient's level of hypnotic susceptibility.

Once the surgeon or the anesthesiologist has determined the ability of the subject to receive hypnotic suggestions, he must determine next how effective hypnotic anesthesia will be for his patient. This process also can be extremely time-consuming as it involves several steps. The conscientious hypnotist first will use several sessions to teach the patient how to relax. During these sessions the patient is taught to enter a very deep state of relaxation and to make himself as comfortable as possible. He is asked to make his limbs feel loose and limp. Further instructions may include procedures outlined by Barber and DeMoor (1972). The employment of these procedures should result in a patient being most receptive to hypnotic anesthesia instructions. The procedures include defining the relaxation sessions as hypnosis. Barber and Calverley (1964, 1965a) found that with such instructions, relaxation was more complete and the subject was more cooperative in following suggestions from a hypnotist. Thus, if the patient is led to believe that the relaxation sessions involve hypnosis and the patient believes in the process of hypnosis, a hypnotic state is more easily achieved and relaxation is more complete.

Hypnotic anesthesia also can become easier to achieve if fears and misconceptions concerning the procedures are removed. During this phase of preparation the patient is assured of the positive benefits of hypnosis and of its safety. If fears and misconceptions still remain, the hypnotist tries to find the reasons and to work through them. The patient also is told that the entire procedure is very relaxing and that the experience will be most pleasant.

After removing possible fears concerning hypnosis, the hypnotist tries to secure the most cooperation possible from his patient. For hypnotic anesthesia to be beneficial, it is necessary that the patient be highly motivated and as cooperative as possible in paying attention to the suggestions of the hypnotist. If complete cooperation is not achieved, hypnotic anesthesia cannot possibly be of much help in reducing surgical pain.

Barber and DeMoor also report that hypnosis is most easily achieved when the subject is instructed to keep his eyes closed during the entire induction procedure. Such instructions appear to play a role in removing visual distractions, in enhancing the subject's ability to imagine vividly and to engage in fantasy, and in augmenting responsiveness to some types of suggestions. Hypnotic anesthesia becomes easier to produce if distractions to the subject are minimized. Keeping the eyes closed helps with this process.

Barber and Calverley (1965a, 1965b) report that when subjects were given suggestions of relaxation, sleep, and hypnosis, responsiveness to other suggestions was far easier to achieve. They believe these results were achieved because such a situation tends to promote the willingness to accept suggestions by producing greater motivation and more positive attitudes and expectancies.

Maximizing the phrasing of suggestions and employing appropriate vocal characteristics also appear to help with the induction of hypnosis. Very simple suggestions rarely will produce the effect that the hypnotist wishes to achieve with his patient. A surgeon who plans to use hypnotic anesthesia cannot simply tell his patient, "Your abdomen is numb." He must use very elaborate instructions, usually in a series. For example, instructions of hypnotic anesthesia, let us say in an arm, might progress in the following manner: "I am going to make your arm very insensitive to all sensations. I want you to imagine that your arm has just been injected with novocaine. Now the effect of the novocaine is beginning to spread throughout your entire arm. You can feel your arm becoming numb, very, very numb. The sensations and feelings you normally experience are leaving your arm. Your arm is becoming more and more numb. It is becoming totally free of all feelings and sensations. Your arm feels as if it were a piece of rubber, as if it were just hanging on to your body, void of all sensations." Such instructions usually will achieve the desired effect.

In addition, the manner in which the instructions are given is very important. Barber and Calverley (1966) found that permissively worded instructions tended to be more effective than those worded authoritatively. However, Garrett and Bloom (1975) recently found that this is not always the case. They discovered that permissive instructions worked best with nonauthoritarian individuals while authoritative instructions worked best with authoritarian subjects. Thus, the mode of delivering instructions to subjects and the success of such instructions in producing a desired hypnotic effect can vary with the subject's personality. Also, vocal characteristics of the hypnotist such as intonations, inflections, and volume can influence the ability of a subject to cooperate with the suggestions of a hypnotist (surgeon) before the administration of anesthesia (Barber and Calverley, 1964).

Coupling hypnotic suggestions with naturally occurring events also has been shown to enhance hypnotizability. In dealing with hypnotic anesthesia this is not easy to achieve. However, if the hypnotist wishes the subject to experience eyelid heaviness and drowsiness, for example, he can couple this suggestion with the naturally occurring event of the subject feeling drowsy as a result of listening to monotonous sources of auditory information, such as the voice of the hypnotist or a monotonous sound source in the same environment with the subject. It also should be possible to couple this desired effect with perhaps naturally occurring arm heaviness or tiredness if hypnotic anesthesia is to be used for arm surgery. However, how does one couple such a suggestion for hypnotic anesthesia when surgery is to be performed on the abdomen? It is apparent that the coupling of a naturally occurring event with a desired hypnotic effect can be difficult to achieve.

Another procedure that appears to enhance hypnotizability is stimulating goal-directed imagining. When given hypnotic suggestions, subjects typically are not asked to carry out an overt action. Rather, they are asked to imagine a situation in which the desired effect would occur. For example, in a previously mentioned case concerned with arm anesthesia, the subject was told to imagine that his arm was injected with novocaine. He then was further instructed to imagine that his arm was completely numb and devoid of all sensations (feelings).

Spanos (1971) studied the relationship between goal-directed imagining and responding to suggestions from a hypnotist. In most instances he found that subjects who best followed hypnotic suggestions reported that they were imagining a situation which, if it actually were to occur, would produce the behavior that was suggested. Subjects who are most capable of this type of imagination are most likely to profit from the use of hypnosis as an anesthetic during surgery.

If hypnotic anesthesia is to be used during surgery on a given patient, the hypnotist must determine at some point if the anesthetic is effective. To accomplish this he must challenge the patient to feel sensations after hypnotic anesthesia has been administered. If the arm has been anesthetized, he may prick the skin of the arm with a needle and ask the patient if he experienced any sensations. Often patients say "no" but show overt signs of pain, such as flinching or grimacing. In these circumstances the anesthesia obviously is not complete and further suggestions of anesthesia and numbness are required. The point that is most important here, however, is that such an experience may make the patient feel that hypnotic anesthesia will not work for him, when, in fact, this may not be the case. Consequently, it is important that the subject's perception of failure be handled in an adequate and professional manner. This can be accomplished by the hypnotherapist telling the subject that his reaction was perfectly normal and that the procedure was necessary for determining how much more anesthesia would be required to totally eliminate all sensations from the arm. The patient should accept this explanation, after which the hypnotist can proceed to induce a stronger hypnotic anesthesia effect. When testing again for strength or presence of anesthesia, it is important that any experiences of failure on the part of the subject be dealt with in a positive, nondiscouraging manner.

The optimal test for determining the presence of hypnotic anesthesia would be one in which the subject did not always have to be pricked. If another procedure could be employed on some occasions, failure experiences could be minimized. Such a procedure was recently discovered (Wallace and Garrett, 1973, 1975; Garrett and Wallace, 1975; Wallace, 1976). Using a simple proprioceptive task in which each subject was asked to locate the tip of his nose with the forefinger of his dominant hand and with his eyes closed, researchers discovered that every subject who had his dominant arm hypnotically anesthesized performed differently from the subjects with normal arm sensations. When the arm was anesthesized, a proprioceptive error was produced. Thus, under hypnotic anesthesia, when a subject was asked to point to his nose, he initially missed the location by four to thirteen centimeters. He located his nose only after a short period of time. Such errors were not made by those with normal sensations in the arm (no anesthesia).

The inability to perform the nose-touch task accurately

and expeditiously usually is indicative of spinal damage. However, those subjects who showed nose-forefinger incongruency while under hypnotic anesthesia showed no such error when hypnotic anesthesia was absent from the dominant arm. Therefore, the inability of a presumably hypnotically anesthetized subject to perform the nose-touch task accurately was taken as a novel test of the presence of hypnotic anesthesia. This procedure could be used in some situations to determine the presence of such anesthesia without pricking the subject's skin with a needle. However, use of this procedure is obviously limited, as it can be applied only to tests of the presence of anesthesia in an arm. Perhaps, in the future, similar tests can be discovered and employed to determine the presence of hypnotic anesthesia in other parts of the body.

Although the absence of this simple proprioceptive ability is interesting, this behavior cannot be employed as the sole determinant of the presence of hypnotic anesthesia. Since the major purpose of such anesthesia is to reduce sensations in a specific body part, the ultimate test to determine if such anesthesia is present obviously is to apply an instrument such as a needle to the skin in different locations around the presumably anesthetized zone. A failure to respond painfully (i.e., show no flinching or painful grimaces) to the needle is a good sign that anesthesia is present. It should be mentioned that even with hypnotic anesthesia the subject is able to feel the pressure of instruments applied to the skin but that this pressure is independent of experienced pain. Pressure sensations should be thought of as normal and not indicative of the absence or incompleteness of hypnotic anesthesia.

After the hypnotist has concluded the preliminary analyses of whether hypnotic anesthesia would be appropriate for a given patient about to undergo surgery, a rehearsal stage of anesthesia is initiated. In this phase the hypnotist may teach the patient a procedure known as "glove anesthesia" (Kroger, 1963). This procedure is basically simple to teach to those deemed sufficiently susceptible to hypnotic suggestion. The primary reason for teaching it is to allow the subject to experience hypnotic anesthesia in a location of the body other than the one on which surgery will be performed. Once this experience has been established and developed, the subject will have a good idea of what to expect in the way of sensation absence during stages of surgery.

Glove anesthesia initially involves the removal of sensation from a patient's hand. This type of anesthetic is administered in a manner comparable to the previously outlined instructions for producing anesthesia in a subject's arm: namely, the subject receives a set of elaborate, detailed instructions and suggestions that his hand is becoming very, very numb. He is told that all the sensations he normally experiences in his hand will be removed, and that his hand will come to feel as if it had received a massive injection of novocaine. He is told that the hand will feel as if it were a total rubber mass, devoid of all sensations. When it appears that the subject has taken to the glove anesthesia instruction, the hypnotist may prick the skin to determine if sensations have been removed sufficiently so that the subject feels no pain. Some subjects will take this suggestion quite readily while others will require several additional sessions to acquire this ability.

Once glove anesthesia has been learned by the subject, he is told that he will be able to transfer the anesthesia to other parts of his body simply by applying his anesthetized hand to that location. The patient then is requested to apply his anesthetized hand to the part of his body on which surgery will be performed. He is told that all sensations will vanish from the touched location. If they do not disappear completely, the patient is requested to keep his hand applied to the location until sensations have vanished totally. The subject then may be informed by the surgeon that should some sensations still be present, that this is quite normal and that under no circumstances will they be permitted to remain during actual surgery—a reduced amount of a chemical anesthetic will remove any remaining sensations. The subject then is further assured that the operation will be completely painless and that he will consider it a pleasant experience.

Before surgery, a "dry run" of the operation may take place (Anderson, 1957; Kroger, 1963). In this procedure the patient experiences what will occur during actual surgery, except no incision will be made. The mock operation commences with a cleansing or sterilization of the area on which surgery will be performed. This is accomplished by applying alcohol with a sponge to that area. The surgeon then stretches the skin of the area and as he makes a mock incision with the light stroke of a pencil or some similar instrument, he informs the patient that the incision is being made and that he should relax. He is told that he will feel absolutely nothing except a little pressure from the instrument, that under no circumstances will he experience any pain. The patient then is informed that his breathing is becoming slower and slower, deeper and more regular. The surgeon tells the patient that the incision has been made and that he will feel absolutely no sensations. Relaxation suggestions are continually given to the patient throughout the mock surgical procedure. This helps the patient remain in the deepest possible state of hypnosis and allows the surgeon to proceed as if a chemical anesthetic had been employed.

During and after the mock surgery, it is important that the hypnotist remain present to continually reinforce previously learned and maintained suggestions. If it appears that the patient can perform adequately in following hypnotic anesthesia and relaxation instructions during the mock surgery, it is likely he will be able to do so during actual surgery. It is important to remember that several mock surgeries may be required to familiarize some patients with the surgical as well as the hypnotic anesthesia procedures. Also, the more presurgical trials one employs, the more relaxed and confident the patient becomes about being operated on with the use of hypnotic anesthesia.

Throughout the actual surgical procedure, the hypnotist is present for several reasons. The patient may require continual reinforcement of the relaxation suggestion. He also may require additional suggestions concerning the absence of pain during surgery. If pain has not been totally eliminated and the patient begins to show discomfort, a reduced amount of a chemical anesthetic is administered by the anesthesiologist during the surgical procedure.

Following actual surgery with hypnotic anesthesia, the patient must be brought out of hypnosis. This is accomplished in a slow and careful manner to make the experience as comfortable as possible. The patient usually is told that he feels as if he is awakening from a very deep sleep. He is told that he will feel very, very relaxed. The hypnotist then will enable the patient to become more relaxed by asking him to perform some task which will shift his attention away from the surgery. The task usually is something quite simple, such as counting from one to one hundred or vice versa. While this task is being accomplished, the patient is given the suggestion that each number counted makes him feel more and more relaxed. The patient is told that he will feel completely relaxed at the conclusion of the counting task. If any pain remains from the surgery, he is told to apply glove anesthesia to the painful area, if he was taught this practice. If it was not taught, a mild analgesic agent and/or a sedative might be given to the patient to help him relax and sleep following the hypnotic debriefing.

Basically, this is the procedure for using hypnotic anesthesia in surgery. It is a safe and valuable tool to help the surgeon and patient during an operation. As was previously mentioned, however, hypnotic anesthesia is not a panacea for the removal of pain during surgery. Often it is used in conjunction with a chemical anesthetic and permits reduced levels of such an agent to be used during an actual surgical procedure. As this is the case, it obviously would reduce the possible side effects inherent in chemical anesthetics and would allow for safer surgery to take place for a patient who shows susceptibility to hypnotic suggestion. So, what once was considered to be "sheer foolishness" by many of Esdaile's colleagues during the 1850s, the earliest years of the use of hypnotic anesthesia, now is a standard procedure used by many surgeons and anesthesiologists for the relief of a patient's pain during surgery. Unfortunately, only a very small portion of the population can adequately undergo surgery without the administration of some chemical anesthetic. However, as was mentioned in chapter 2, hypnotic susceptibility level is not a constant and can be improved with proper training. Therefore, it is possible that most individuals can be taught to take a hypnotic anesthesia suggestion before and during surgery to reduce the dosage of chemical anesthetic to be administered. The benefits of reducing the chemical anesthetic dosage already have been mentioned and cannot be overemphasized, especially in terms of the safety factor.

Obviously, the procedure for inducing hypnotic anesthesia is rather long and tedious even for those sufficiently susceptible to hypnosis, and longer still for those requiring further hypnotic training. For these reasons, many surgeons currently do not employ hypnotic anesthesia as an alternative or as an adjunct to chemical anesthesia, although there are enough to make the procedure available for patients. In a recent survey (Pulver and Pulver, 1975) of 101 alumni of a course in medical hypnosis, 75 percent indicated that they had used some hypnotic techniques in their medical practices. However, hypnosis was used primarily for nonsurgical and nonanesthetic purposes. It is doubtful, therefore, that hypnotic anesthesia will be a widely accepted and often used procedure for surgery in the near future. Currently, it is used most often for patients who are allergic to chemical anesthetics and patients whose generally poor health or advanced age makes the use of chemical anesthetics dangerous.

Hypnosis and Obstetrics

Another contemporary use of hypnotic pain relief is in the field of obstetrics. As in the field of general surgery, the use of hypnotic anesthesia and analgesia in childbirth is not new. It was used as a means of reducing childbirth pains over 100 years ago (Kroger, 1963).

As with all uses of hypnosis, first it is necessary to determine the level of hypnotic responsiveness of the patient. If the expectant mother is deemed sufficiently susceptible to hypnotic suggestion via some of the tests suggested in chapter 2, she can be trained to accept hypnotic anesthesia and analgesia suggestions before and during parturition. However, it should be noted that, as with general surgery, only a small percentage (about 20 to 25 percent for childbirth) of patients can effectively be taught to reduce the severity of pain without the assistance of some chemical anesthetic or analgesic.

Most women who have given birth with the aid of hypnotic analgesia have done so by choice. Many who wish to do so, however, learn prior to parturition that hypnotic anesthesia and analgesia simply will not suffice as a pain relief measure for them. As a result of going through some hypnotic training sessions, however, these patients do become more cooperative and relaxed during childbirth (Tom, 1960).

For those who can profit by the use of hypnotic analgesic and anesthetic suggestions in childbirth, the advantages are considerable. These were enumerated by Kroger (1963) and include: (1) the reduction of fear, tension, and pain before and during labor; (2) the reduction or elimination (for extremely good hypnotic subjects) of the chemical anesthetic dosage level; (3) the complete control of uterine contractions during childbirth; (4) a speedier recovery; (5) a lack of undesirable postoperative effects such as would be encountered with chemical anesthetics; (6) a reduction in the first stage of labor by two to three hours; (7) an elevation in the resistance to fatigue following parturition; (8) an easy substitute for chemical anesthesia for those individuals showing allergies to such drugs; (9) benefits for premature deliveries; (10) the fact that hypnotic anesthesia instructions can be given by the husband with very little training from a hypnotist, thereby making the wife more relaxed during childbirth; (11) no possibility of danger to the mother or the baby (This is extremely important as it has been demonstrated that chemical anesthetics administered to the mother interfere with the oxygen supply to the fetus which could result in brain damage to the fetus.); and (12) a more pleasant experience for the mother than with chemical anesthetics because with hypnotic anesthesia the mother can "enjoy" the first cry of the baby and see him immediately after birth.

Kroger (1963) also lists some disadvantages of hypnotic anesthesia and analgesia in obstetrics. These are as follows: (1) it is successful in the relief of pain in only 25 percent of patients without an accompanying chemical anesthetic; (2) hypnotic induction and maintenance may be affected in the labor room by exposure to the cries of other women in various stages of labor; (3) it is time-consuming compared to chemical anesthesia; (4) a trained hypnotist usually must be available during the entire labor period; and (5) misconceptions about hypnosis in general prevent many patients from profiting by its use as an anesthetic.

With the aforementioned advantages and disadvantages in mind, it can be seen that the advantages far outweigh the disadvantages. Consequently, hypnotic anesthesia could be thought of as an adjunct or a possible substitute for chemical anesthesia during childbirth.

As with hypnotic anesthesia in surgery, the use of such anesthesia in obstetrics also requires extensive preparation and training on the part of the patient. First the expectant mother should be informed of the beneficial effects of such methods of pain relief. Then, during the third or fourth month of pregnancy, hypnotic anesthesia and analgesia conditioning should commence. Approximately fifteen to twenty sessions at the obstetrician's office are required for the patient to learn such phenomena as "glove anesthesia" (previously described with regard to surgery). The fifteen to twenty sessions typically are divided into two or three sessions per month until birth. If it is discovered that the patient cannot achieve glove anesthesia within eight to ten sessions, it is presumed that hypnotic anesthesia and analgesia will not be sufficient to reduce pain during labor and childbirth.

Each patient capable of performing glove anesthesia is instructed to transfer this anesthetic effect to another part of her body (usually a side of her face). This enables her to see that sensations can be reduced or eliminated. Then the patient typically is instructed to transfer the feeling of numbness to her abdomen. During the transference process, the hypnotist continually reinforces feelings of relaxation and comfort by suggesting that with each breath the patient takes she is becoming more and more relaxed and more and more anesthetized. Kroger (1961) has suggested that a posthypnotic suggestion also be given that anesthesia can be transferred to the perineum at the appropriate time.

When the hypnotist is confident that the patient is learning hypnotic anesthesia and transference adequately, he will test various anesthetized sites to determine the presence and strength of such anesthesia. If the hypnotist is fairly certain that hypnotic anesthesia will be beneficial for the patient, as determined in manners similar to those previously described for surgery, the patient is so informed. Then she is required to continue hypnosis sessions with the obstetrician until she is ready to give birth. This serves to continually reinforce her ability to perform glove anesthesia and transference of anesthesia.

In addition, the patient is instructed to use hypnosis as an analgesic during labor through autohypnosis. She is taught this procedure along with the previously mentioned procedures during the fifteen to twenty hypnosis sessions with the obstetrician prior to labor. If self-hypnosis cannot be mastered, a hypnotist or the husband, if sufficiently trained, must be present during labor to aid the patient in the relief of pain.

As is evident, hypnotic anesthesia and analgesia are important, beneficial tools in the field of obstetrics. However, is it possible that many of the beneficial effects achieved with hypnosis also could be achieved with "natural childbirth" methods? This possibility has been considered by several investigators.

Hypnotic Anesthesia vs. Natural Childbirth Preparation

Davenport-Slack (1975) recently compared and evaluated childbirth with hypnosis and childbirth with antenatal training, including Read's Natural Childbirth method, the Lamaze method, the Psychoprophylactic method, and Jacobson's Progressive Relaxation technique. Generally, she concluded that both types of procedures were similar in producing the desired effects during labor and parturition: namely, a reduction in the severity of experienced pain. In addition, both hypnosis and antenatal training have been shown to produce greater relaxation (Jacobson, 1959) in patients. Both methods generally have been found to shorten the length of labor (August, 1965; Miller, 1961; Ringrose, 1966), to allow for a reduction or elimination of medication (Pascatto and Mead, 1967; Huttel, et al., 1972), to reduce behavioral signs of pain (Tanzer, 1967; Kroger, 1961), and to increase the positive aspects of the childbirth experience (Davenport-Slack and Boylan, 1974). With regard to the latter beneficial effect, mothers reported childbirth with hypnosis or with one of the natural childbirth procedures to be "fantastic" and "mystical" (Tanzer, 1967).

When hypnosis has been used as an analgesic and an anesthetic during childbirth, it often has been assumed that women experience a marked reduction in the subjective experiences of pain. This also was stressed as being the case with the use of natural childbirth procedures. However, few studies have asked women to rate their experienced pain during labor or childbirth with natural childbirth procedures (Davenport-Slack and Boylan, 1974; Javert and Hardy, 1951). In neither of these studies did natural childbirth preparation appear to affect subjective experiences of pain. No studies could be found that compared subjective pain during childbirth with and without hypnotic preparation. Thus, there is little empirical evidence to support the contention that all childbirth pains will disappear with either hypnotic or natural childbirth preparation. These methods, however, do eliminate some of the associated pain, making childbirth a more pleasant experience for the mother.

Hypnosis and Dentistry

Another beneficial use of hypnosis is in the field of dentistry. Although it can be used as a local anesthetic in lieu of procaine or novocaine, this is not its most common use. Most dentists who employ hypnosis in their practices use it to reduce tension or fear and to allow the patient to relax. The result of this is that the magnitude of experienced pain is reduced. Such pain is strongest when the patient is most tense.

Again, as with all uses of hypnosis, first it is necessary to determine how readily the patient can be hypnotized. Simple susceptibility tests such as arm rigidity or the hand clasp can be used. Once this is accomplished, the patient can be acquainted with the desired use of hypnosis for his treatment. If hypnotic anesthesia is to be used, the dentist might first try glove anesthesia. In this way he can determine if the patient can take to hypnotic anesthesia. If he can, the patient then can be instructed to transfer such anesthesia to his gums and to areas proximal to the desired location where dental work is to be performed. Some dentists employ direct hypnotic anesthesia to the desired location without teaching the patient glove anesthesia. In either case, it is desirable that the patient be seen by the dentist or oral surgeon several days before the scheduled operative procedure. This is necessary to familiarize the patient with the dental procedures of hypnotic anesthesia and to reduce the magnitude of fears and anxieties associated with dental work in general.

In dentistry, the benefits of hypnotic anesthesia over chemical anesthesia are as great for the suitable patient as in general surgery. These advantages were outlined by Moss (1963) and include: (1) the elimination or reduction of the patient's tensions, anxieties, and fears of pain (This allows the patient to be more relaxed during dental procedures and, perhaps, experience less pain.); (2) the maintenance of the patient's comfort during long periods of dental work; (3) the reduction or elimination of chemical anesthetics or analgesics; and (4) the establishment and maintenance of postoperative anesthesia.

In addition, hypnosis has been employed in dentistry in the conditioning of patients to wear a prosthetic or orthodontic appliance. Often these devices are initially uncomfortable and sometimes produce irritation and slight pain. Hypnosis can be employed in such situations to reduce the magnitude of the experienced discomfort.

As is apparent, hypnosis is as beneficial a tool in dentistry as it is in surgery and obstetrics. Unfortunately, as with surgery and obstetrics, not all individuals are readily hypnotizable and, therefore, not all patients can profit by the beneficial effects of hypnotic anesthesia.

Hypnosis and Headaches

As an analgesic, hypnosis has been of great value in the treatment of one of man's most common pain complaints, the headache. Two methods of hypnotic analgesia have been employed to deal with headaches: glove anesthesia and the hand-warming technique.

Glove anesthesia is used for headaches in much the same way it is used for surgery, obstetrics, and dentistry: namely, the patient is taught the glove anesthesia procedure, if he is found to be readily hypnotizable, and he is instructed to apply his hypnotically anesthetized hand to his head at the onset of a headache. As sufferers of headaches cannot always go to the doctor at each onset, they also can be taught to induce glove anesthesia by autohypnosis. This usually will require several visits to the hypnotist (doctor) to learn the correct technique. This includes learning to become very, very relaxed—far more relaxed than during the normal waking state. This is accomplished by teaching the patient to concentrate all of his attention on a single thought (fantasy) or object. If focused attention is learned by the patient and relaxation results, the individual can be taught to self-induce glove anesthesia and apply it to the headache.

Headache sufferers, however, often have extreme difficulty in learning to become relaxed and in applying self-induced glove anesthesia. When this is the case, the patient's spouse, parent, or trusted acquaintance can be taught to administer the anesthesia procedure. Unfortunately, such an individual may not always be present when the patient experiences a headache. Therefore, teaching the patient self-hypnosis and proper methods of relaxation is the most beneficial method if hypnosis is to be used for the relief of pain associated with headaches.

Another technique employed for headache relief is the hand-warming procedure (Sargent, Green, and Walters, 1973). In this method the patient receives instruction concerning the use of something called a "temperature trainer" which indicates the differential temperature between the midforehead (a common location for headaches) and the right index finger. The patient is taught to achieve passive concentration and to relax his entire body with hypnotic procedures. He is given the hypnotic suggestion that his hands are becoming warm. This suggestion is repeated as often as is necessary, until the patient "feels" his hands as being warm. Then he is instructed to visualize the changes in his hands while watching the temperature trainer. This indicates whether the subject can increase the temperature of his hands relative to his forehead. In this manner, the patient thinks about making his hands warm and, in fact, they become warm. Sargent, et al. suggested that with this procedure blood flow to the hands was decreased. This was associated with a decrease of blood vessel constriction, a possible contributor to migraine headaches. With this hand-warming technique, Sargent, et al. reported a considerable improvement in a majority of their migraine patients. Graham (1975) and Andreychuck and Skriver (1975) found similar, positive results in their patients.

Thus, it appears that hypnotic analgesia is very beneficial for the control and alleviation of headaches. As with previously described uses of hypnotic anesthesia and analgesia, the use of hypnosis with headaches also has some distinct advantages. It can substitute for chemical analgesics such as aspirin, Bufferin, Tylenol, and Datril. Also, since many headaches are psychogenically influenced by tension and anxiety, hypnosis and biofeedback techniques such as those employed by Sargent, et al. eventually can help the patient reduce in magnitude or eliminate completely the occurrence of such headaches. This is not possible with chemical analgesics which only temporarily raise the patient's pain threshold.

In addition to the use of hypnotic analgesia for headaches, it also has been employed for other types of pain such as that associated with arthritis, rheumatism, and cancer. Here, too, glove anesthesia can be employed. As these diseases involve extensive and chronic pain and suffering, hypnotic anesthesia would be of great benefit to the patient in helping him cope with the pain. It is unlikely that hypnosis can be used to remove pain totally in these instances, as the pain is physiologically or biologically determined. Therefore, hypnosis is used, typically in combination with chemical agents, to help reduce the magnitude of the pain and to allow the patient to cope with his suffering.

As is apparent from the described applied uses of hypnotic anesthesia and analgesia, great benefits can be derived from their use in the relief of pain. Unfortunately, as was previously mentioned, only a minority of individuals can profit maximally from such pain relief measures in lieu of chemical agents. However, many can adequately be trained (given enough time and patience on the part of the hypnotist, be he a surgeon, an obstetrician, a dentist, an anesthesiologist, or a general practitioner) to increase their levels of hypnotic susceptibility, if only temporarily. If the hypnotic susceptibility level can be increased and the patient can be trained to accept a suggestion of hypnotic anesthesia or analgesia, this would permit for the combined use of hypnosis and reduced chemical means for the relief of pain. As hypnotic techniques are the safest known means of relieving pain, the potential benefits of this procedure are enormous.

5

Sexual Dysfunction and Hypnosis

IN RECENT YEARS much has been written and discussed concerning sexual functioning and dysfunctioning in today's society. Specifically, a topic which not long ago was considered almost taboo, now is receiving a great deal of attention. Also, individuals and couples who once were afraid or embarrassed to turn to a professional for advice on a sexual matter now are avidly seeking such counsel. What are the sexual problems for which individuals are seeking help? Currently, what therapies are available for the treatment of psychologically based sexual problems? Can hypnosis be of assistance in the treatment of any sexual disorders? These are some of the questions that will be answered in the course of this chapter.

Sexual Dysfunctions

Generally, sexual disorders classified as psychologically induced fall into several categories, according to Masters and Johnson (1970, 1975) and Kaplan (1974, 1975). These include the male dysfunctions referred to as impotence and ejaculatory incompetence and the female dysfunctions referred to as orgasmic dysfunction and vaginismus.

Male impotence refers primarily to the inability of a male to achieve and/or maintain an erection. This dysfunction is generally classified into two types: primary impotence and secondary impotence. In the former, maintenance of an erection adequate for successful sexual intercourse does not take place. In the latter, an erection does occur on certain occasions, but not on others. Secondary impotence is the more common form of this disorder.

Two types of male ejaculatory incompetence exist. These are premature ejaculation and retarded ejaculation. The former type refers to the inability to control ejaculation long enough for insertion and/or maintenance on insertion. As a result, the partner does not achieve sexual satisfaction. Retarded ejaculation refers to the inability to ejaculate after insertion.

The most common female sexual problem is orgasmic dysfunction. There are two forms of this disorder. The first is sometimes referred to as psychological frigidity or primary orgasmic dysfunction. In this disorder the female is completely devoid of any sexual feelings during foreplay or during actual intercourse. The second form of orgasmic dysfunction is situational in nature: the female attains normal orgasmic responses during sexual stimulation or intercourse under certain circumstances, but not under others.

Another female sexual dysfunction is vaginismus. In this disorder, penetration by the male is difficult, if not almost impossible, because the muscles at the entrance to the vagina experience an involuntary spasm. As a result, the female is said to "freeze up", producing constriction of the vaginal opening.

If a given sexual dysfunction has been diagnosed by a physician as being nonorganic in origin, its cause according to Kaplan (1974) and Coleman (1976) can be: (1) insensitive, incompetent, and ineffective sexual techniques by one or both partners during foreplay and intercourse, (2) feelings of fear, anxiety and inadequacy, (3) interpersonal problems, (4) the changing male-female roles in today's society and/or (5) homosexuality. Many of these causal factors of sexual dysfunction have been treated successfully with a form of sex counseling approximating or identical to that of Masters and Johnson (1970).

Treatment

Basically, the treatment program of Masters and Johnson consists of three parts: (1) an extensive and thorough medical examination of both partners to rule out the possibility that dysfunction may be the result of organic problems, (2) a training program in which each partner learns to experience pleasure in caressing the other's body and genitals in extended foreplay without intercourse, and (3) prescribed sexual experiences and therapy, the nature of which is determined by the type of sexual dysfunction being treated.

With the use of this sex therapy program, Masters and Johnson have reported considerable success with their patients. For vaginismus the therapy success rate was 100 percent. For premature ejaculation the success rate reported also was remarkable (98 percent). On the other hand, the success rate for primary impotence was only 59 percent. Of all the sexual dysfunctions previously enumerated, the overall average rate of treatment success was 80 percent. This is a remarkable "cure" rate for any disorder, especially for sexual dysfunctions which are nonorganic in nature.

Although Masters and Johnson's treatment program is very successful with regard to sexual dysfunctions, one wonders whether behavior modification and/or hypnosis could be employed beneficially in the treatment of such dysfunctions. Since systematic desensitization with the aid of hypnosis has been successful in the treatment of anxiety resulting from such disorders as phobias and obsessive-compulsive behavior (see chapter 3), could this dual approach also be used in the treatment of sexual dysfunctions? As many sexual disorders are produced by or associated with anxiety, systematic desensitization coupled with hypnosis might prove quite beneficial. In fact, Fuchs and his colleagues (Fuchs, Hoch, and Kleinhauz, 1976; Fuchs, et al., 1973) report several instances of the beneficial use of systematic desensitization with hypnosis in the treatment of vaginismus. These researchers consider vaginismus an avoidance reaction to an anxiety-producing situation, namely, sexual intercourse. Basically, two approaches have been used to treat this sexual dysfunction. Fuchs and his collaborators refer to these methods as the "in vivo" technique

and the "in vitro" technique. In the former method the patient
is taught self-hypnosis to produce a state of body relaxation.
The patient then is encouraged to insert her finger in her
vagina to aid with dilation of the opening. Following this
procedure, prelubricated dilators of gradually increasing size
are inserted to further help expand the opening. This insertion procedure also is performed by the attending physician
and by the patient's mate. This enables the patient to deal with
insertion by others.

All insertions by the "in vivo" technique are performed in
the patient's home as well as in the physician's office. Such insertions occur while the patient is in the supine and in the
female-superior position. With this technique the patient
gradually learns to relax and to accept the insertions. The
female-superior position will become the recommended position for eventual sexual intercourse. In general, this "in vivo"
procedure has been found to be fairly successful in the treatment of vaginismus.

A second procedure for dealing with vaginismus is the "in
vitro" method. This technique requires first that the patient be
hypnotized. Then a hierarchy of anxiety-provoking events
with sexual connotations is established. (The establishment of
such a hierarchy is described in chapter 3 with regard to the
treatment of phobias.) The therapist then asks the patient
under hypnosis to produce vivid imagery of events as they are
described to her in succession from least to most anxiety-provoking. With each presentation, the patient is asked to feel
very, very relaxed. If anxiety does not result, she continues to
run the gamut to the strongest possible anxiety-producing
event, namely, sexual intercourse. This "in vitro" technique is
practiced in the physician's office as well as in the patient's
home. In general, this technique, as the "in vivo" technique,
has proved to be very useful in the treatment of vaginismus.

Several case studies by Fuchs and his co-workers can more
effectively illustrate these techniques. In the case involving the
use of the "in vitro" technique, a twenty-three-year-old woman
reported that after two years of marriage sexual intercourse had
not taken place, primarily because she feared the pain it might
involve. As a result, her vagina did not allow for the insertion

of her husband's penis. She had seen a gynecologist concerning this problem who determined that her dysfunction was psychologically induced. She eventually was referred for hypnotherapy.

Hypnotherapeutic treatment of the "pain fear" during intercourse commenced with the establishment of a detailed history of her sex education and her knowledge of sexual matters. Error or misinformation, where noted, was remedied by appropriate explanation.

Following the initial interview with the patient, her level of hypnotic susceptibility was established. Since the patient was found to be susceptible to hypnotic suggestion, hypnosis was used for two purposes: to help the patient achieve a state of relaxation and to help her produce vivid imagery of events which the physician would describe to her.

After it had been established that the patient was able to relax and produce imagery with the aid of hypnotic suggestion, a stimulus hierarchy was presented under hypnosis. The patient was given the hierarchy of events in order from least to most anxiety-provoking. Advancement up the hierarchy depended upon first achieving relaxation at a lower level. The hierarchy of events presented to this patient was as follows: (1) imagining herself going home with her husband and resting with him, (2) imagining herself as being tired and retiring with her husband in the bedroom (no sexual activity involved), (3) imagining herself caressing, petting, and embracing her husband, (4) imagining herself in a love-play situation with her husband, (5) imagining herself undressing in front of her husband, and (6) imagining herself having intercourse with her husband without fear.

It is important to emphasize that in progressing through the steps of the above hierarchy, advancement was not made unless the patient assured the therapist that she felt relaxed with the imagined situation. Also, at this point, it should be mentioned that Fuchs and his co-workers found that five therapy sessions were typically necessary from the initial interview to the achievement of relaxation through this part of the hierarchy.

Once relaxation had been achieved with the above suggested imageries, more situations were described and suggested to the patient under hypnosis. In a sixth therapy session these included the following imagined situations: (1) being in bed with her husband, (2) observing her husband's body and sexual organs, and (3) experiencing friction of her sexual organs with those of her husband. Upon achieving relaxation with these suggestions, the patient was asked under hypnosis during a seventh session to imagine: (1) herself undressed, in bed with her husband, and engaged in foreplay, (2) friction of sexual organs, and (3) penetration of the head of her husband's penis.

During an eighth session, suggestions of full and actual intercourse were imagined by the patient. These imagery situations were repeated over and over again until the patient responded that she did not feel anxious about the imagined experiences. The intercourse suggestions were repeated in a ninth session. Following this last session, the patient reported that she finally had been able to experience sexual intercourse with her husband without experiencing any pain. Thus, hypnosis teamed with systematic desensitization was successful in the treatment of vaginismus for this patient.

If vaginismus is more severe than in the above case study, Fuchs and his co-workers employ their "in vivo" therapy. This therapy was used with a nineteen-year-old female who complained of excruciating pain whenever her husband had attempted to insert his penis in her vagina. As with the previous case study, first a history of the sexual problem was established. It was learned that in two and one-half years consummation of the marriage had not taken place, and that the husband had stopped trying to have intercourse with his wife because it gave her so much pain.

Following the initial interview with the patient, she was requested to come to a workshop for self-hypnosis instruction which, at the time, was being taught to pregnant women preparing for natural childbirth. During this session the patient learned to experience self-hypnosis.

On a subsequent visit, the patient was given a gynecological examination before which she was asked to hypnotize herself for the purpose of achieving relaxation. After the brief examination, she was requested to and agreed to insert one of her fingers in her vagina. While in her relaxed state with the aid of hypnosis, she was assured that there would be a marked absence of pain. She subsequently was introduced to a set of instruments which are used to dilate the vaginal opening. She was requested to start with a dilator approximately equal in width to her finger. After success was achieved with the first dilator, she was asked to proceed with dilators of increasing width, until she easily could accommodate a dilator approximating the size of an average erect penis.

Following the insertion of dilators in the physician's office, the patient was instructed to take a dilator home and to introduce it while in a female-superior position and to practice this procedure for several days. During this procedural exercise she was to use self-hypnosis to help her relax.

Subsequently, the patient's husband was contacted and was asked to visit the physician's office. He was told that intercourse should be attempted with his wife, using the female-superior position. This position was to be employed so the patient could take the initiative and feel more relaxed knowing she was not being "attacked" by her husband. She also could control speed and depth of penetration. Using this procedure, the couple reported success with sexual intercourse for the first time in two and one-half years. There no longer was any associated pain.

Using hypnosis as a relaxant in the "in vivo" technique and as a relaxant plus a means of producing vivid imagery in the "in vitro" technique, Fuchs and his colleagues reported remarkable success in the treatment of vaginismus. With the former procedure, a 67 percent success rate was found, and with the latter, 90 percent.

It appears that vaginismus can be treated successfully with procedures employing hypnosis as an aid. Hypnosis also has been found to be useful in the treatment of primary and situational orgasmic dysfunction. Wickramasekera (1976) considers these forms of psychological frigidity as instances of sexual anesthesia. In other words, the reason some females do not experience orgasm is because of the absence of sexual sensations in their genital regions. If this is the case, it should be possible to remove the anesthetic effect with the aid of hypnosis so that sensations are "restored." Wickramasekera reports that such treatments have been successful for some of his patients.

Nuland (1976) employed hypnosis in the treatment of secondary male impotence. This dysfunction usually is accompanied by extreme trauma and anxiety and, if not treated, could lead to a more serious form of psychological impotence, namely, primary impotence. Secondary impotence generally is treated as a dysfunction produced as a result of fear. This fear is reduced in magnitude and nature by hypnotic relaxation in a manner similar to that employed by Fuchs and his colleagues in the treatment of females for vaginismus. By using the sex therapy methods of Masters and Johnson plus hypnosis to facilitate imagery and relaxation, Nuland reports success in the treatment of secondary male impotence.

Unfortunately, the use of hypnosis has not been consistently successful in the treatment of induced, secondary impotence or for primary orgasmic dysfunction. In a report of several case studies by Segal (1970), he states that the use of hypnosis for his patients made a doubtful contribution to a remission of their dysfunctions. However, his report seems to indicate that hypnosis was employed more casually than in studies reporting its successful use in the treatment of sexual dysfunctions. That is, Segal did not employ hypnosis for the purpose of producing vivid imagery or deep relaxation. It was used only as a very mild relaxant. Therefore, it is not surprising that his use of hypnosis was not as successful as others have reported it to be.

Erickson (1973) has applied hypnosis to the treatment of premature ejaculation. A patient, thirty-eight years of age, sought hypnotic treatment of his sexual problem after a series of unsuccessful attempts at treatment by several physicians and after the unsuccessful use of prescribed medications and commercially advertised remedies and devices. This individual described a long history of failures in sexual intercourse with normal dates and with prostitutes because of premature ejaculation before coitus. One instance exemplified the severity of his problem: after six months of dating a girl without having any sexual encounters with her, he kissed the girl and immediately ejaculated in his pants.

Although the patient generally felt that hypnosis probably would be of little help to him, he was willing to try it as a last resort. Therapy was begun by inducing a light trance which moved to a deep trance in which the first two of three posthypnotic suggestions were given: that he must obtain a wristwatch with an illuminated dial and a second hand, and that in the future he always would wear his watch when he happened to be in bed.

He was instructed to continue seeing girls in his usual manner. It was explained to him that this would be necessary in his therapy. Following this explanation, the third posthypnotic suggestion was given. It went as follows: ". . . Do you realize, do you understand, are you in any way aware, that your premature ejaculation will end in a failure, that no matter how long your erection lasts, no matter how long and actively you engage in coitus, you will fail to have an ejaculation for 10, for 10 long, for 15 long minutes, for 20, for 25 minutes? Even more? Do you realize how desperately you will strive, how desperately you will watch the minute hand and the second hand of your wristwatch, wondering, just wondering if you will fail, fail, fail to have an ejaculation at 25 minutes, at 25½, at 26, at 26½ minutes? Or will it be at 27½, at 27½ minutes—at 27½, at 27½ minutes?

"And the next morning you still will not believe, just can't believe, that you won't fail to have an ejaculation, and so you will have to discover again, if you really really can have an ejaculation, but it won't be, it can't be, at 27½ minutes, nor even at 28, nor even at 29 minutes. Just the desperate hope will be in your mind that maybe, just maybe, maybe at 33 minutes, or 34, or 35 minutes the ejaculation will come. And at the time, all the time, you will watch desperately the wristwatch and strive so hard lest you fail, fail again, to ejaculate at 27 minutes, and then 33, 34, 35 minutes will seem never, just never, to be coming with an ejaculation.

"And now, this is what I want you to do. Find one of the girls you are used to. Walk her to your apartment. When you come to the corner (before you turn to go into your apartment), even as you turn right try so very hard to keep your mind on the conversation, but notice that you can't help counting one by one the cracks in the sidewalk until you turn into the courtway and step upon the boardwalk. With com-

plete intensity you are to try hard, very hard to keep your mind
on the conversation, but keep counting desperately the cracks,
the cracks between the boards, the cracks under you, all those
cracks all along the way to your apartment until it seems that
you will never never never get there, and what a profound relief
it will be to enter, to feel comfortable, to be at ease, to give your
attention to the girl, and then, and then, to bed, but not the
usual—but the answer, the real real real answer, and from the
moment you enter the apartment your mind will be on your
wristwatch, the watch that, as time goes by, can at long last,
bring you the answer.

"Quickly now, keep all that I have said in your unconscious mind—locked up, not a syllable, not a word, not a
meaning forgotten—to be kept there, used, obeyed fully—then
you can remember just me and come back and tell me that the
wristwatch was right when it read 27½ minutes and when it
read 33, 34, and 35.

"Arouse now, completely rested and refreshed, understanding in your unconscious mind the completeness of the
task to be done (Erickson, 1973, pp. 220-221)."

Three days after this final posthypnotic suggestion with
amnesia was given, the patient reported that he no longer
experienced premature ejaculations. In fact, he asked if it was
not unusual to have postponed ejaculation in coitus 27½ to 33
minutes after penetration. He was assured that this was not
unusual. Therapy was considered to be quite successful in
treating his specific problem.

Thus, it appears that hypnosis can be used successfully in
the treatment of premature ejaculation, as well as other sexual
dysfunctions previously discussed. Often hypnosis is used in
conjunction with other behavioral therapies, specifically systematic desensitization, in the treatment of dysfunctions associated with anxiety or fear. These include vaginismus and
secondary male impotence. Other dysfunctions such as premature ejaculation and orgasmic dysfunction have been treated
successfully with the use of hypnosis alone.

The fact that hypnosis has proved to be useful in the
treatment of sexual dysfunctions leads one to ask whether it
also can be useful in enhancing sexual excitement. For example, might hypnosis be useful for a male not clinically diag-

nosed as a premature ejaculator, in postponing ejaculation for a sufficient period of time after penetration to permit mutual orgasm with his partner? If Erickson's premature ejaculation therapy could be employed for this purpose, the answer would probably be "yes." In addition, it also might be possible to induce a numbness in the penis during coitus through the use of self-hypnosis. This type of hypnotic anesthesia performed with the glove anesthesia technique (see chapter 4) possibly could allow a man to prolong coitus sufficiently to time his orgasm (ejaculation) with that of his partner. At the proper time, the anesthetic effect could be removed to permit normal ejaculation.

In conclusion, hypnosis appears to be a useful therapy in treating some nonorganic sexual dysfunctions. It is not as widely used as Masters and Johnson's therapy, nor is it as successful. However, where it has been employed, especially when other therapies have failed, it has proved to be useful.

6

Habit Control

IN THE PAST few years we have heard much about various methods of controlling unwanted habits; such as overeating, smoking, and excessive alcohol consumption. As each of these habits has been shown to produce various medical problems— high blood pressure, diabetes and heart disease (for overeating), emphysema and lung cancer (for smoking), and cirrhosis of the liver and heart disease (for excessive alcohol consumption)—many individuals have sought methods of treatment to help them reduce or eliminate their specific habit. Some of these methods include psychotherapy, behavior modification, and hypnotherapy. Which of these methods is least "painful" in terms of time spent in treatment and the amount of work required by the patient? These questions and others will be explored in this chapter.

Overeating

Individuals who find themselves overweight often wish that they could shed some of their excess pounds. In addition to the health reasons specified above, reasons given for wanting to lose weight include: (1) the inability to fit into previously comfortable clothes; (2) the inability to find dates or mates (Excessively overweight individuals generally have a more difficult time procuring dates than well-proportioned individuals.); and (3) the feeling that the extra pounds make them look ugly. This latter reason, undoubtedly, is related to the second reason.

How have individuals attempted to lose weight? The obvious choice has been to diet. There are a countless number of diets one could attempt. Basically, the type of diet is not as important as the goal—to lose weight. It is in dealing with a weight loss that most individuals experience the greatest difficulty. Choosing a diet is often very simple and staying on the diet for a few days is within the grasp of most individuals. Losing a few pounds, theoretically, should act as a reinforcement to continue on the diet. However, for many individuals, this is not always the case. They become tired of their diets (self-imposed or recommended by a physician) and wish they could eat the foods they enjoyed most and in the quantities they once savored. At this point, the individual may return to his former eating habits. If this does occur, the vicious cycle starts anew. The person gains weight or remains heavy, wishes he could lose weight, goes on a diet, gives up the diet, and so on. This cyclical process could go on indefinitely.

If an individual finds himself in the "eating cycle," perhaps dieting, in and of itself, is not sufficient. He may need some outside help. If the person realizes that this is the case, he may seek such assistance from a physician. First, it is important to rule out any medical causes for obesity, such as a malfunction of the neural regulation of the feeding and satiety centers, a malfunction of the glucostatic mechanism associated with control of the appetite, or an aberration of lipid and adipose metabolism (Kroger, 1970). If the weight problem is diagnosed as resulting from psychological factors, the physician puts the patient on an appropriate diet and may recommend a psychologist trained in problems of obesity. The trained specialist, if consulted, may employ one or more therapies to help the obese individual to stay on a diet and eventually to lose weight.

After a given diet is specified for an individual, either in terms of food types or quantities or both, a therapy may be incorporated into the diet maintenance procedures. The most commonly employed therapies are behavior modification and hypnotherapy. One or both may be employed in conjunction with the patient's dieting.

One of the major goals of diet control therapies, besides helping the patient lose weight, is to determine the underlying reasons for the individual's excessive eating. Is overeating preceded by anxiety or depression? If so, why is the patient anxious or depressed? Obviously, the process involved in determining the underlying reasons for overeating could be time-consuming. Moreover, the discovery of the reasons for overeating does not automatically give the patient insight into his problem and enable him to stop overeating. If the patient's problem of obesity could be solved that easily, it would be a minor miracle.

There are many reasons why individuals overeat. Some overeat to alleviate boredom, depression, and anxiety; some, because food simply tastes good and they enjoy eating; others, because of a variety of reasons. Discovering a patient's specific reason or reasons is important, as this information can be used in the development of a weight-reducing plan.

Once the reasons for overeating have been established, the patient may be asked to set a weight-loss goal. For example, a patient weighing 200 pounds may be asked, "How much would you eventually like to weigh?" If the patient responds with a figure such as 160 pounds, that is established as the goal. The attainment of this goal is considered adequate, even though medical charts may indicate that 135 pounds would be the best weight level for him. The final weight goal is entirely up to the patient.

After a weight goal is established, the eating habits of the patient are determined. For instance, at what time of day does overeating become most intense? When is overeating least intense? These are important questions, as their answers can help determine procedures to be used in aiding the patient to lose weight. For example, if it is learned that a patient overeats most while sitting at home alone and watching television, this gives the psychologist, as well as the patient, some insight into situations which most reinforce overeating. Does the patient overeat least when occupied with house work (vacuuming, dusting) or with other time-consuming chores? Again, this probing produces valuable information which can lead to an effective weight-reducing program.

The psychologist and the patient then may discuss an individually based program to initiate and maintain a weight loss. One such procedure makes use of techniques referred to under the rubric, behavior modification (Mikulus, 1972). In the control of obesity, these techniques basically involve the rewarding of appropriate diet behavior and/or the punishing of overeating behavior. Thus, a reward system may be introduced for a demonstrated weight loss. This is accomplished by setting a reward to be obtained once a weight-loss goal has been achieved.

For example, let us say that an individual wishes ultimately to lose forty pounds. The physician or psychologist managing the behavior modification of overeating activity may ask the patient to set intermediate goals which, when achieved, will be rewarded. For instance, with each five-pound weight loss, the patient's mate rewards this person by taking him or her to an enjoyable social event, such as a movie or a concert. This rewarding continues until the total forty-pound weight-loss goal is achieved. Should the patient gain weight during the program or even after the program, the reward system also can be employed in reverse: if weight is gained, the reward is withdrawn. In this case, the patient's mate ceases to take him or her to any social events until the weight is brought back to the originally established level. Using this system, weight loss is rewarded and weight gain is punished.

Behavior modification as a therapy in helping individuals reduce their weight level has been fairly successful (Kennedy and Foreyt, 1968; Stuart, 1971; Wolpe, 1969). Stunkard (1973) also reports a history of success with this therapy. One example he cites is of an individual whose roommate rewarded him for a weight loss by assuming the unpleasant tasks of washing dishes or taking out the garbage. A second example concerned an overweight husband. In his case, his wife refused to have sexual intercourse with him on any day that he did not lose weight. After a desired weight loss had been achieved and maintained by both of these patients, treatment was terminated.

Another technique that has been employed with weight control through behavior modification includes what is referred to as a "point system." With this approach an individual is required to earn a certain number of points by maintaining a previously established diet plan. In one case reported by Stunkard (1973), these points were converted into money. This money eventually was given to a charitable organization of the patient's choice. The more weight he lost, the more money his charity received. The earning of little or no money with this procedure was supposed to induce guilt on the part of the patient, and make him strive to lose weight so he could contribute money again. This technique obviously would not work well unless the patient could afford to donate money to a charitable cause, could be made to feel sufficiently guilty if donations were small or nonexistent, and could be made to perceive the entire weight-loss-donation contingency as meaningful and important. As a matter of fact, with this technique, there appears to be a high attrition or dropout rate, ranging between 20 and 80 percent. Also, many who lose weight with this procedure eventually regain a major portion of it (Stunkard, 1958). In addition, only 25 percent of those who enter treatment lose as much as 20 pounds and only 5 percent lose 40 pounds or more (Stunkard and McLaren-Hume, 1959). The reported weight loss achieved with this technique appears to be indicative of the average weight loss reported with behavior modification, in general. So, regardless of contingencies, the greatest weight loss that can be expected with any behavior modification technique appears to be around 40 pounds (Stuart, 1967). However, this is generally regarded as successful.

The major difficulty in relying totally upon behavior modification as a means for controlling weight is that learned procedures for weight control are amenable to extinction: that is, contingencies developed between behavior and a reward do not always maintain a strong tie; what was at one time rewarding may not always be so rewarding.

Given the difficulties attendant upon the sole use of behavior modification principles and techniques, hypnotherapy has been employed to help individuals deal with obesity (Erickson, 1960). As with all uses of hypnosis, before this procedure can be employed beneficially, first it is necessary to determine whether an individual can readily be hypnotized. If a patient has been found to be susceptible to hypnotic suggestion, hypnotherapy can be used by itself (Erickson, 1960) or in conjunction with behavior modification techniques (Kroger, 1970).

Erickson describes several case studies in which hypnotherapy was used to help a patient lose weight. In one study, a woman weighing 240 pounds sought hypnotherapy in an attempt to reestablish her normal weight level of 120 pounds. She explained to the physician that all attempts to help her reduce to her normal weight had been futile. A case history of the patient revealed that her primary reason for eating great quantities of food was that she enjoyed food so much—it gave her immense gustatory or taste pleasure. The more and the longer she ate, the better the food tasted.

As the patient was found to be highly susceptible to hypnotic suggestion, she was instructed with regard to a task termed time distortion. In this procedure, the psychological concept of time is changed in such a manner that, for example, a minute may seem like an hour. She was instructed that, henceforth, she was to eat all meals in a state of time distortion. Although Erickson does not specify, this procedure presumably was made possible through a posthypnotic suggestion wherein the taste of food triggered time distortion. Consequently, as the patient completed tasting and eating each portion of food, both her sense of taste and feelings of hunger were completely satisfied, as if she had been eating for a far longer period of time. With this procedure the patient was able to lose 120 pounds over a period of nine months without any medical complications. Also, the weight loss was maintained.

In a second case, Erickson reports the history of a woman who, when first seen, weighed 270 pounds. Her weight ought to have been between 130 and 140 pounds. As in the previous example, the patient reported a history of failures in all attempts to lose weight. She had heard that hypnosis might help her and she came to Erickson as a last resort. Instead of employing time distortion therapy as in the previously described case, Erickson allowed the patient to continue overeating in a hypnotherapy program, but she was instructed (under hypnosis) to overeat only enough to support a given weight level. For example, at first she was instructed to overeat enough to support 260 pounds. At each session thereafter, the therapist asked the patient to overeat to support a lower weight level. The program continued until she "overate" enough to support 190 pounds. This weight loss occurred within a six month period after the initiation of hypnotherapy.

In this example, overeating for the sake of overeating appeared to be the patient's primary problem in gaining weight. It would have been extremely difficult to extinguish this highly reinforced behavior with a conventional approach; Erickson did not attempt this. Instead, he continued to reinforce overeating, but at a continually lower level, using hypnotic suggestions of weight goals. With these "overeating" suggestions and the aid of hypnotherapy, the patient managed to lose weight.

Kroger (1970) has used hypnotic glove anesthesia in the treatment of obesity. (This technique was described in chapter 4.) To treat the problem of overeating and hunger, glove anesthesia is applied to the epigastrium or stomach region whenever a hunger contraction occurs. The patient simply places his "numbed" hand over this location and hunger contractions are minimized. As a result, the patient eats less food. However, this technique is only situationally successful. It would not be beneficial, in and of itself, as an obesity control technique for patients who eat regardless of the presence of hunger or hunger contractions.

Obviously, not all patients can successfully lose weight solely with the use of hypnotherapy. Primarily this is due to the fact that not all patients are highly susceptible to hypnosis. Erickson has stated that his patients were highly susceptible. If a patient is only moderately susceptible to hypnotic suggestions, does this preclude the use of hypnotherapy in the control of his obesity? The answer is no. However, hypnotherapy probably would have to be paired with behavior modification therapy for such patients. This dual approach has been used successfully by Kroger (1970). Furthermore, it has been reported (Platonov, 1955) that, in general, learned or conditioned behavior established under hypnosis is more durable and less likely to go into extinction. Thus, it would appear that this dual approach to the treatment of obesity is probably the most viable of all, since it is not dependent upon the subject being extremely high in hypnotic susceptibility. However, it still requires the subject to be hypnotizable for the behavior modification therapy sessions.

Smoking

Another habit which has been treated and controlled successfully with hypnosis is smoking. Each year many individuals who smoke attempt to eliminate this habit through a variety of means—cutting down from a high number of cigarettes smoked to a smaller number, substituting some other habit for smoking such as chewing gum, or going "cold turkey" and quitting the smoking habit entirely. However, many of those who attempt to stop smoking experience a great deal of difficulty. Some find that cutting down on the number of cigarettes smoked per day does not lead to the elimination or control of the habit. Those attempting to substitute another habit for smoking may find themselves developing an equally aversive habit, such as overeating or increased alcohol consumption. In addition, the smoking habit eventually can return to be shared with newly developed, aversive habits. The attempt to stop smoking entirely without any help or substitute often is extremely difficult and few individuals are able to stop smoking in this way.

As the most commonly employed methods for controlling or stopping smoking appear to produce less than desirable results, what alternatives does the smoker have to control this habit? One possible solution involves the use of hypnosis. As with all uses of hypnosis, first it is necessary to determine how susceptible an individual is to hypnotic suggestion. However, being susceptible to hypnosis is not enough; it also is necessary that the person be motivated to stop smoking. An unwill-ingness to give up smoking for any of a number of reasons will prevent him from stopping. If an individual enjoys smoking and does not wish to terminate the habit, the use of hypnosis or any other means of dealing with habit control will meet with failure.

Often a concerned spouse or relative will try hard to persuade a smoker to stop smoking. This effort is virtually futile and will undoubtedly meet with failure if the smoker does not wish to abandon his habit. Furthermore, asking the individual to seek a professional to aid him in giving up smoking will be equally as futile if there is no desire to stop smoking. Therefore, the persons who will profit most from the use of hypnosis in the elimination of a smoking habit are those who both wish to give up smoking and are readily susceptible to hypnotic suggestion.

Basically, two hypnosis strategies have been employed in dealing with the smoking habit: inducing gustatory dissatis-faction or making cigarette smoking literally distasteful and presenting a competing response to smoking.

The first method in dealing with the smoking habit often effects only a temporary cure. This procedure involves the suggestion to subjects that the taste of cigarette smoke will become unpalatable, even extremely distasteful. If a subject is deemed readily hypnotizable, the hypnotist may suggest to him under hypnosis that cigarette smoke no longer will taste pleasant, but rather, very bitter, for instance, as bitter as quinine, and that with each puff, the taste of the cigarette will become more and more aversive. In terms of the distasteful suggestion, the possibilities are limitless. The type of aversive taste suggestion is chosen at the discretion of the hypnotist.

Following the distasteful suggestion, the subject is asked to light a cigarette and smoke it. The first puff or two may not produce much in the way of results. However, shortly thereaf-ter, the subject begins showing signs that the taste of cigarette smoke is becoming aversive. He may begin coughing, chok-ing, and/or become nauseated. He is asked to continue smok-ing regardless of the annoying side effects. He may obey this suggestion temporarily, but refuses soon after, as the taste of the cigarette smoke becomes more aversive. At this point the subject is allowed to discontinue smoking.

The person who shows signs of following the aversive gustatory suggestion of the hypnotist can be given a posthypnotic suggestion: namely, lighting cigarettes in the future will produce the same aversive sensations experienced in the hypnosis session. To determine if the posthypnotic suggestion is effective, the subject is asked to light and smoke a cigarette as he is about to leave the therapist's office. If the experience is as distasteful as in the hypnosis session, the therapy is considered to have been successful.

However, at this point, it should be mentioned why this anti-smoking procedure is limited, even with respect to the group designated as most able to profit from the use of hypnosis. Even though the taste of cigarette smoke becomes aversive as a function of hypnotic suggestion, this aversion lessens with time. Thus, the terrible taste becomes less terrible with time, until the subject has adapted to the once aversive gustatory sensation. As a matter of fact, this situation is analogous to the first few times the subject smoked at all, perhaps as a teenager. When he lit his first cigarette and tasted smoke, he probably coughed, choked, and may have felt nauseated. With time and practice, however, these initial side effects decreased in intensity and eventually disappeared. So, when a hypnotist suggests to a subject who smokes that the smoke will be distasteful, the hypnotist merely is recreating for the subject a situation which existed in the past. Since he learned to adapt to the taste of cigarette smoke originally, he is likely to adapt again, this time to the hypnotically induced gustatory sensation. Both experiences produce distasteful gustatory and other sensations to which one adapts with time, eliminating once-present side effects.

In addition to the possible adaptation to the aversive gustatory sensations produced with hypnotic suggestion, another consequence of such suggestion may be the presence of a generalized discomfort, coughing, and nausea when anyone smokes in the presence of the subject. Thus, the side effects of smoking may occur even when the subject himself is not smoking, but rather when others are smoking near him. This is not a desirable situation and even when it is suggested to the subject during hypnosis that he will not experience such side effects, the incidence is still prevalent.

As an alternative to the gustatory technique in controlling smoking behavior, Spiegel (1970) has suggested a competing response procedure. After a subject has been hypnotized, he is asked to concentrate on the following three points: (1) cigarette smoking is a poison to his body, (2) life is not possible without his body, and (3) life is possible only if the subject respects and protects his body. These three points constitute a procedure that Spiegel introduces to compete in strength with the habit of smoking. In essence, then, two habits are competing with one another. One habit is that which the smoker is attempting to eliminate, namely, cigarette smoking. The other "habit" is developed by the subject from birth and is strengthened via suggestion during a hypnotherapy session. This "habit" is life itself. Since most subjects obviously would prefer life over cigarette smoking, the former habit should win the competition. If the subject continually reinforces his life habit over his cigarette habit, the latter habit may extinguish and the subject will stop smoking. However, if the smoking habit is reinforced by the continuation of smoking behavior, this act, in essence, serves as a punishment for the continuation of the life habit and smoking cigarettes will continue. So, the subject is confronted with a life-or-death dilemma in Spiegel's technique. If he chooses to continue smoking, he decreases the life habit. If he stops smoking, he increases the life habit.

How successful has Spiegel's technique been in the treatment of the smoking habit? He reports that with a large sample of 615 subjects, 20 percent succeeded in terminating their smoking behavior in a single-treatment session. In addition, Spiegel's procedure is reported to be successful even without a hypnotic induction procedure if a subject is sufficiently motivated to stop smoking. However, it is most successful when hypnotic suggestion is employed.

Often, those who have terminated the smoking habit have blamed this termination for the development of an equally aversive habit, such as overeating. Does this occur when

Spiegel's technique is employed? Although he reports that some subjects did commence overeating with the termination of smoking, others lost weight. The majority of the 20 percent success group experienced no weight gain or weight loss. In general, Spiegel's competing habit technique did not produce new, equally aversive habits.

An appropriate question can be posed at this point with regard to Spiegel's technique. Is 20 percent a successful cure rate for smoking? Spiegel believes that it is, as a 20 percent cure is better than no cure. Can this cure rate be increased? Spiegel offers several suggestions that might increase it. These include increasing the number of hypnotherapy sessions for smoking control and encouraging public figures to refrain from smoking in public. The former suggestion appears to have some encouraging support from Hall and Crasilneck (1970) who report a 75 percent cure rate with four hypnotherapy sessions. With regard to public figures smoking in public, Spiegel believes that because these individuals are highly imitated, they indirectly encourage their admirers to smoke. If these public figures would discontinue their habit, at least in public, it could encourage or motivate their admirers not to smoke, according to Spiegel.

Many principles of behavior modification are employed by Spiegel to treat the smoking habit. Is it possible then that the use of behavior modification without hypnosis can be as beneficial as hypnotherapy? The answer appears to be "yes." In a review of studies in which the smoking habit was treated solely with behavior modification techniques (Bernstein, 1969), many successful attempts at control are delineated. However, as Dengrove (1970) points out, hypnosis can act as an important catalyst to keep the patient sufficiently motivated and encouraged to eliminate the smoking habit.

Alcohol Consumption

In addition to the use of hypnosis in the treatment of overeating and smoking, hypnotherapy has been applied to the treatment of excessive alcohol consumption. Basically, the techniques that have been employed in the treatment of alcoholism are similar to those used in the treatment of the smoking habit. A commonly employed technique is to make the taste of alcohol unpleasant with the aid of hypnotic suggestion. For this method to be effective, it is necessary, as with all techniques for the control of habits, that the individual wishes to rid himself of excessive alcohol consumption. If he does not, no technique will be effective. In addition, it is necessary to determine if the prospective patient is readily hypnotizable. If these requisites are met, there is a good chance that hypnotherapy can be used effectively.

Hypnotic taste suggestions can be used in the treatment of alcoholism, as in the treatment of cigarette smoking. It can be suggested to the patient during hypnosis that alcohol will taste and smell extremely unpleasant. Some unpleasant tastes may include warm soapy water or straight quinine water. In essence, any unpleasant taste or smell suggestion will suffice. Kroger (1963) has suggested that the patient be allowed to establish his own unpleasant taste and smell suggestion by responding to the request that he associate alcohol consumption with "the most horrible, repugnant smell and taste . . . ever experienced" (p. 270). The patient is taught that this taste suggestion will always be associated with alcohol consumption. For this technique to be maximally effective, the patient must be taught autohypnosis or the ability to induce his own hypnotic taste suggestion in the absence of the therapist. This is necessary since the patient will not always be able to go to the therapist when the suggestion must be induced.

As with the taste suggestion in the control of cigarette smoking, such suggestions usually are only temporarily effective in the control of excessive alcohol consumption. Techniques which have been shown to be more effective include the conditioned reflex technique (Kroger, 1942) and group hypnotherapy (Kroger, 1963).

The conditioned reflex technique involves the inducement of a nausea-producing reaction to alcohol consumption: whenever the patient drinks, he will experience nausea. This association is produced initially within the confines of the therapist's office. First the patient is asked to consume some alcohol in the presence of the therapist. While this occurs, the nausea-producing agent is administered. Shortly thereafter, the patient experiences nausea which culminates in vomiting. If this association is developed between alcohol consumption and vomiting, eventually the patient will become ill in the absence of the nausea-producing agent and alcohol itself will produce nausea. This conditioning technique has been successful in about 24 percent of the patients in such therapy (Wallerstein, 1958). As one might expect, this technique, as well as the taste suggestion technique, is most successful at the early stages of therapy. With time, however, the strength of the conditioned reflex (nausea) wanes and, consequently, so does the success of the therapy.

Is it possible to introduce a substitute for alcohol to take the place of drinking? The answer is yes. However, one must be sure that the substitute is not equally averse. Excessive eating, smoking, the taking of drugs are not viable substitutes for alcohol consumption. Acceptable substitutes may include the consumption of soft drinks (preferably sugar-free drinks so that the patient does not gain weight while eliminating alcohol) and chewing gum (also, preferably, sugar-free). As with the taste suggestion, however, habit substitution is successful for only a small percentage of patients.

Another technique that has been found to be fairly successful in the treatment of alcoholism is group hypnotherapy. Wallerstein (1958) reports that this procedure has been successful with about 36 percent of patients involved with alcohol consumption control. Also, Beahrs and Hill (1971) and Byers (1975) report success with the group hypnotherapeutic approach in the treatment of alcoholism. In this treatment procedure, the taste aversion technique and other procedures previously delineated can be employed. Although it was mentioned that these techniques do not achieve striking success in individual therapy, they appear to become far more potent in a group setting. Observing many individuals becoming ill from the aversive taste suggestion vicariously increases one's own distaste for alcohol. In addition, patients freely discuss their alcohol consumption problems with one another. This helps bolster the individual's motivation for terminating alcohol consumption and leads to a more successful therapy in the treatment of alcoholism. This aspect to the treatment has

been employed successfully for many years by Alcoholics
Anonymous. The advantage of hypnotherapy, however, is that
it incorporates suggestions into the therapy which, with the
aid of hypnosis, make the therapy more potent and motivating.
Thus, the techniques employed by Alcoholics Anonymous
would probably be even more effective if strong, motivating suggestions concerning the elimination of alcohol consumption were to be incorporated into their group discussions.
Basically this is what is accomplished with group
hypnotherapy.

A method not yet employed with alcoholism but which
deserves some attention is Spiegel's (1970) competing response
technique. This method was described previously with regard
to the treatment of the smoking habit. If it were to be employed
with alcoholism, one would merely substitute "alcohol" as the
"poison to the body" in place of "smoking." As in the control
of smoking, it is likely that this technique would be successful
with some patients in the treatment of alcoholism.

In addition to the treatment of excessive eating, excessive
alcohol consumption and smoking, habits such as fingernail
biting and thumb-sucking have been controlled successfully
with hypnotherapy. The techniques employed with such
habits are similar to those previously described and used with
other habits. Thus, the aversive taste suggestion can be
employed with fingernail biting or thumb-sucking. Or it can
be suggested to the subject under hypnosis that such behavior
is extremely immature and not befitting his age. If the subject
is ten years old, for example, it is unlikely he wishes to be
associated with a younger age set: e.g., "If you suck your
thumb you are acting like a baby." However, if he continues
this behavior, this will be the case. With these competing
responses he must choose between thumb-sucking with associated immaturity and no thumb-sucking with associated
maturity. This technique has been used successfully by this
author in treating fingernail biting and thumb-sucking. However, as with smoking, overeating, and drinking, long-term
success depends upon the motivation of the patient and the
willingness to eliminate the habit. Without the presence of this
motivating factor, no method of therapy, including hypnosis,
can be successful in the control of unwanted habits.

7

Information Processing and Hypnosis

STILL ANOTHER APPLIED use of hypnosis is in the study of processes such as memory and perception. Hypnosis has been used to restore memories of past events and experiences using hypnotic age regression and to expand, via hypnotic time distortion, the processing time of information to be learned. In addition, hypnosis has been applied to perceptual processes, such as visual acuity activity and visumotor coordination. These perceptual processes and memory manipulations will be considered in this chapter.

Hypnosis and Memory

One of the most remarkable demonstrations of hypnosis in the study of memory is age regression. Hypnotic age regression involves the process of taking a subject back in time. For example, an individual can be taken back to the age of six to have him recall events which happened to him during that period of time. In so doing, he may be asked to remember, for example, what he did on his sixth birthday.

Several studies (True, 1949; Parrish, Lundy, and Leibowitz, 1969; Walker, Garrett, and Wallace, 1976) have demonstrated the restoration of previously learned processes or the memory of past events with the use of hypnotic age regression. Before a discussion of these experiments, however, a brief description of the process of inducing hypnotic age regression is in order.

Hypnotic age regression can be induced by several different means. A common induction involves a counting procedure, which begins with a hypnotized subject being asked to specify his age. Let us say the person replies that he is eighteen years old. The hypnotist then informs the subject that starting from this age, a countdown will take place from eighteen to a given number, and that each number, as it is spoken, will represent the passage of a year of time. The hypnotist then begins counting and stops at the desired age, for example, of six. Once this point is reached, the hypnotist begins questioning the subject to determine if age regression has occurred. This typically is indicated by the recall of information from that point in the individual's life or the initiation of some types of childlike behavior (e.g., rudimentary handwriting or voice changes).

Using this process, True (1949) age-regressed subjects to eleven, seven, and four years of age. At each of these points, he asked them to name the day of the week on which their birthday occurred. True found that with age regression, 81 percent of his subjects correctly named the day.

Unfortunately, several attempts at replicating True's results have met with failure (Barber, 1961; Fisher, 1962; O'Connell, Shor, and Orne, 1970). A possibility for this failure to replicate has been given by Barber, Spanos, and Chaves (1974): namely, True may have known before the experiment the day on which a given individual's birthday had occurred. Subjects were to name this day in answer to the hypnotist's questioning technique, e.g., "Was it Sunday? Was it Monday?" The possibility that True was aware of the correct answer may have affected his tone of voice and inflections when he asked the questions, thereby subtly indicating the correct answer to subjects. Thus, True may have biased his results. In addition, Barber (1962) has suggested that one can calculate a specific date if he knows that the days of the week go backward one day each year and two days in a leap year. It appears, then, that True may not adequately have controlled his experimental paradigm to substantiate the reality of hypnotic age regression.

A second study which manipulated age regression via hypnosis was conducted by Parrish, Lundy, and Leibowitz (1969). Their goal was to determine if age-regressed adults would exhibit perceptual processes similar to those exhibited by children. Two visual illusions were shown to children and adults. Without hypnotic age regression adults perceived the illusions differently from children. However, when adults were age-regressed, the perception of the illusions matched the normative data from actual children. On the basis of these results, Parrish, Lundy, and Leibowitz concluded that "age regression facilitates the use or nonuse of visual cues and mechanisms in a manner typical of earlier stages of perceptual development" (p. 693). Unfortunately, as with the study by True, attempts at replicating this finding have met with failure (Ascher, Barber, and Spanos, 1972; Porter, et al., 1972).

A third experiment which employed hypnotic age regression to study a process that changes from childhood to adulthood was undertaken by Walker, Garrett, and Wallace (1976). They investigated a phenomenon known as eidetic imagery or photographic memory. Basically, eidetic imagery involves the ability to examine a visual stimulus, such as a design or a picture, for a brief period of time and later to project this formed image onto a neutral surface or to close one's eyes and remember the details of the initially perceived stimulus. This ability has been shown to exist in about 8 percent of the childhood population (Haber and Haber, 1964). However, the process is virtually nonexistent in adults. Therefore, a good test of eidetic imagery in adults regressed to the age at which this process is most apparent (seven years of age). If age-regressed adults display photographic memory, this would be a strong demonstration of the value of hypnotic age regression in recovering past abilities and memories.

The results of the Walker, Garrett, and Wallace study, in fact, demonstrated that age regression was successful in recovering the ability of some adults to use photographic memory.

Two of twenty age-regressed subjects successfully demonstrated eidetic imagery abilities. In a postexperimental interview it also was learned that these two individuals had faint memories of being able to perform this feat as children. These former childhood eidetikers, then, were able to recover the process with the aid of hypnotic age regression. Unlike the True and Parrish, Lundy and Leibowitz studies, this study could not possibly be criticized for a failure to control experimental situations, as the experimenter did not know either the identification of objects to be recognized or if subjects were or were not hypnotized until after the experimental manipulation. In this study, hypnosis was induced before the experiment commenced by someone other than the actual experimenter. In addition, there was absolutely no way that subjects could have identified the objects without a pair of special spectacles unless they used photographic memory abilities. This was the case because object identification required the merging of two fields of vision perceived independently. It appears, then, that Walker, Garrett, and Wallace have adequately demonstrated the phenomenon of hypnotic age regression and its role in the recovery of past abilities and memories from childhood.

An applied use of hypnotic age regression for the restoration of information can be illustrated by a kidnapping case which occurred in 1976. In this crime a bus driver and twenty-six children were kidnapped while on a field trip in Chowchila, California. When the children and their bus driver were successfully rescued, the driver could not remember the license plate number of the kidnapper's car. However, with the aid of hypnotic age regression to the time of the kidnapping, the driver was able to give law enforcement authorities the correct license plate number. This information helped in the identification of the criminals. Hypnotic age regression, then, appears to be a useful tool for the solution of crimes when helpful information has been repressed due to the trauma of the event. Recall of this information could aid in the eventual arrest of criminals.

Another demonstration of the use of hypnosis in memory involves a phenomenon known as time distortion. This pro-

cess was briefly mentioned in chapter 6. Time distortion with
the aid of hypnosis involves the suggestion to a subject that a
second is perceived to last a minute, a minute is perceived to
last an hour. Consequently, what normally takes an hour to
learn or process may be accomplished in a far shorter period of
time as a result of this time manipulation. Several investigations (Zimbardo, et al., 1973; Krauss, Katzell, and Krauss, 1974;
Garrett, 1975) have shown the potential, beneficial use of time
distortion in the processing of information.

Zimbardo, et al. manipulated time distortion hypnotically
in an attempt to determine if such a procedure would affect the
speed at which a telegraph key could be pressed. Zimbardo, et
al. first taught subjects to press a key at a designated rate.
Afterward, subjects received time distortion suggestions under
hypnosis so that time was perceived as being slower or faster
than the usual experience of time. Normally, one minute is
perceived as lasting one minute; with time distortion, one
minute is perceived as lasting much longer or much shorter
than one minute. With this manipulation, key-pressing
response rates were altered according to time distortion
instructions. Thus, it appears that in this study the perception
of time was altered appreciably with the use of hypnotic time
distortion instructions.

An experiment by Krauss, Katzell, and Krauss (1974) also
considered the effects of hypnotic time distortion on task
performance. Their experiment was concerned with the ability
of subjects to learn information with the use of time distortion.
Three groups of subjects received information to be learned.
One group was given three minutes with no hypnotic time
distortion; a second group was given ten minutes with no
hypnotic time distortion; a third group received time distortion instructions under hypnosis so that three minutes of actual
time was perceived as lasting for ten minutes. Results showed
that the third group performed as well as the second and much
better than the first. It appears, then, that hypnotic time
distortion allowed subjects to learn and process information in
a shorter period of time than normally is required.

In addition to the aforementioned studies, Garrett (1975)
also found hypnotic time distortion to be beneficial in a search

task requiring subjects to locate a simple, geometric shape (e.g., a triangle) embedded in a more complex design. With time distortion, subjects were able to locate such figures in a significantly shorter period of time than when no such manipulation was employed.

It appears that the distortion of time through hypnosis is useful as a tool in expediting the processing of information. In the instances cited, time distortion permitted individuals to perform tasks or to learn information in a shorter period of time than normally is required. The beneficial aspects of this procedure are fairly evident. For instance, subjects capable of being hypnotized readily could be taught to read faster and learn faster. This obviously would be useful in schools for pupils being taught to read and comprehend material. It also would be of considerable help in business settings where individuals are required to process information in short periods of time. However, for practical use in nonlaboratory settings, subjects would have to be taught procedures for self-hypnosis to produce the time distortion.

Hypnosis and Perception

In addition to the potential uses of hypnosis in learning and memory, hypnosis also has been applied to perceptual problems such as nearsightedness (Graham and Leibowitz, 1972; Harwood, 1971): that is, research was conducted to determine if hypnosis could be applied to improve visual acuity.

Graham and Leibowitz employed hypnosis as a means of helping nearsighted subjects relax the muscles around and behind their eyes. When such relaxation was employed along with the practicing of relaxation of eye muscles at home, the combined procedures were effective in producing a marked improvement in visual acuity: namely, subjects who were nearsighted became better able to perceive fine detail in objects and in the environment than before the hypnotic manipulation. In addition, a follow-up on the participating subjects indicated that the manipulation was in effect long after the experiment had been terminated.

In a related study by Harwood (1971) the results of Graham and Leibowitz were replicated. In general, nearsighted subjects showed a 15 percent improvement in visual acuity following hypnotically induced relaxation of the eye muscles. It appears, then, that hypnotically induced relaxation of the oculomotor muscles of the eyes is of some benefit in treating myopia or nearsightedness.

It should be noted, however, that although there was an improvement in the perception of detail following hypnotic eye-muscle relaxation, myopia was not eliminated. Subjects still needed to wear corrective lenses. It is important to realize, though, that hypnosis was beneficial in treating some of the conditions responsible for nearsightedness, notably eye-muscle tension.

In addition to the use of hypnosis to improve visual acuity, hypnosis has been applied to the potential improvement of perceptual and motor skills, such as bowling accuracy and swimming speed. Using hypnosis to induce relaxation and, thereby, reduce tension during sports competition, Garrett (1974) reports that college swimmers showed an improvement in speed after a hypnosis relaxation induction.

With the use of hypnosis as a relaxant, as well as a means of helping subjects focus their attention on the task at hand, Garrett (1976) also reports that bowlers showed improvements in their bowling accuracy. These observations by no means were fully controlled laboratory studies, nor can one be certain that motivating instructions or "pep" talks without hypnosis would not have been equally as effective. However, they do indicate the potential usefulness of hypnosis in the improvement of various perceptual and motor skills involved in such sports as swimming and bowling. In addition, hypnotic relaxation and selective focusing instructions probably could be applied to improve other perceptual and motor skills such as typing accuracy, or accuracy in a factory sorting task or assembly task.

Hypnosis appears, then, to be a useful adjunct in helping individuals process information, whether learning or performing a task in a shorter than normal period of time or improving visual acuity with hypnotic eye-muscle relaxation. Although the research in these areas of study, at present, is rather sparse, further research undoubtedly will uncover many applied uses of hypnosis to help improve human skills and abilities.

8

Hypnosis, Sleep, Dreams and ESP

HYPNOSIS IS CONSIDERED by many to be a state of sleep or, at least, related to the phenomenon of sleep; individuals who are hypnotized are thought to be in a state of consciousness resembling sleep with corresponding physiological stages. Is there any scientific evidence to suggest that hypnosis and sleep are similar states of consciousness? Are dreams that are experienced while in a state of hypnosis related to dreams experienced while asleep? These questions and others concerned with the relationship of hypnosis to sleep will be considered in this chapter.

Hypnosis and Sleep

Since the time when the Marquis de Puysegur (1780s) discovered that a state of somnambulism or a sleep-like trance was present in individuals under hypnosis, many attempts have been made to determine if, in fact, hypnosis is related to sleep. A subject under hypnosis does appear to be in a restful state approximating sleep. This is not surprising when one realizes that most hypnotic inductions typically involve suggestions to the subject such as "you are getting drowsy," "your eyelids are getting heavy," or "you are feeling very, very relaxed."

To determine if hypnosis is related to sleep, it is necessary to physiologically compare states of sleep with the state of hypnosis. The most commonly employed procedure for doing so is to compare the patterns of brain or electroencephalographic (EEG) activity during stages of sleep and during hypnosis. These patterns are recorded by attaching electrodes to various locations of an individual's head; the electrodes detect neural activity from the brain. If it can be established that brain wave patterns during hypnosis approximate patterns occurring during sleep, strong evidence will exist that hypnosis and sleep are either the same or, at least, closely related to one another in a physiological and a behavioral sense.

Before comparing the EEG patterns for subjects who are either asleep or hypnotized, a brief description is in order of what normal or average EEG patterns are like during various stages of consciousness. Six stages of consciousness can be differentiated (Evans, 1972) based on EEG patterns—one waking state and five sleeping states.

The waking state is characterized in terms of EEG pattern by beta waves (high frequency, low amplitude waves) if the subject has his eyes open and is cognitively active, or by alpha waves (lower frequency, higher amplitude waves) if the subject has his eyes closed while awake and basically is not engaging in any particular mental activity. Thus, in the average individual, the waking state is characterized by a mixture of beta and alpha waves.

The first of the sleeping states occurs when the individual becomes drowsy. In terms of EEG activity this stage is characterized by alpha waves which are lower in frequency and lower in amplitude than in the waking state. These waves become increasingly intermittent and lower in amplitude until they disappear.

After alpha waves have disappeared, the second sleeping state occurs. This state is physiologically characterized by high frequency and high amplitude EEG waves. These usually are superimposed on a background of mixed frequency and relatively low amplitude activity.

The third stage is characterized by EEG wave patterns lower in amplitude than alpha waves. These low amplitude waves are known as delta waves.

During the fourth stage the deepest level of sleep occurs. It is characterized by very high amplitude and low frequency waves.

The final sleeping stage basically is a return to the first sleeping stage in terms of produced EEG patterns. However, this stage differs from the first because of the appearance of rapid eye movements (REM). These movements resemble blinking actions with the eyes closed. Such eye movements were discovered to be associated with a period of dream activity (Aserinsky and Kleitman, 1953).

With the aforementioned stages in mind, it should be possible to compare EEG activity during hypnosis with the EEG patterns that occur in waking and/or sleeping states of consciousness. In fact, several investigators have addressed themselves to this issue and have found that EEG patterns during hypnosis appear to be quite different from the EEG patterns of sleep. For example, Jakobson and Kales (1965) found an absence of delta waves during hypnosis, whereas this type of wave is quite prevalent during the third and fourth stages of sleep.

Others have found a tendency for hypnosis EEG patterns to resemble the light sleep EEG patterns of the first sleep stage (Chertok and Kramarz, 1959; Tart, 1965). However, Evans, et al. (1969) have noticed that some subjects have a tendency to fall asleep to a degree while hypnotized; consequently, it is not surprising that hypnotized subjects may exhibit EEG waves resembling the first stage sleep patterns. In general, it would appear that hypnosis and sleep are independent states of consciousness, at least as exhibited and discriminated by EEG patterns.

As Evans (1972) mentions, however, it may be more meaningful to talk about the relationship between hypnosis and specific EEG patterns rather than to try to determine if hypnosis and sleep are one and the same. Several questions can be asked at this point. Do some subjects exhibit different brain wave patterns in the normal, waking state than others? If so, is this pattern difference in any way related to individual levels of hypnotizability: namely, is there a relationship between EEG pattern and hypnotic susceptibility?

There appears to be some evidence that there are individual differences in EEG activity and that such differences are related to hypnotic susceptibility level. London, Hart, and Leibovitz (1968) found that subjects judged to be high in hypnotic susceptibility, as measured by scores on the Harvard Group Scale of Hypnotic Susceptibility (see chapter 2), tended to show more alpha waves during the waking state than subjects scoring low on this scale. This finding was confirmed by Galbraith, et al. (1970). However, further attempts to replicate this phenomenon have been far from successful. For example, Evans (1972) reports that he found no such relationship. He concludes that the contradictory results may be a function of demand characteristics. In the studies reporting the positive relationship, Evans finds that subjects were told that they were going to participate in a study concerned with "hypnosis and brain waves." Under such circumstances, it is possible that subjects built up expectancies with regard to anticipated performance levels. This presumably produced more alpha wave activity in subjects high in hypnotic susceptibility. However, this would be possible only if such subjects were capable of controlling alpha activity.

It so happens that there is evidence to suggest that alpha wave activity can be altered or manipulated by some subjects (Kamiya, 1969). Merinina (1955) reported that subjects high in hypnotic susceptibility showed decreases in the amplitude and frequency of alpha waves during hypnosis. This suggests, of course, that Evans' (1972) conclusion may have been correct: high hypnotic susceptibility is related to the amount of alpha activity because subjects high in hypnotic susceptibility are capable of altering alpha. However, low-susceptibility subjects also are capable of controlling alpha activity. Thus, if demand characteristics are present, many subjects regardless of hypnotic susceptibility level can determine the hypothesis of an experiment concerned with "hypnosis and brain waves"; they could possibly respond to the expectancies of the situation and produce results congruent with the experimenter's prediction.

In summary, it would appear that there is no conclusive relationship between brain activity patterning and hypnosis. Furthermore, alpha activity does not predict hypnotizability. Experiments in which such a relationship has been found appear to have methodological problems in that they have failed to control for possible demand characteristics.

Hypnosis and Dreams

Although it appears that EEG patterns of a hypnotized subject more closely approximate a waking state than a sleeping state of consciousness, it still is possible that hypnosis may be related to sleep in another dimension—dream production. In other words, dreams produced during sleep may be qualitatively similar to dreams or dream-like states produced during hypnosis. If this is the case, it should be possible to determine in an objective manner if a similarity does exist.

Objectively, dreams during sleep are assessed by the presence of REM patterns. These eye movements generally indicate that a subject is dreaming. Do such REM patterns occur when it is suggested to a subject under hypnosis that he will experience dreams, either in his present hypnotic state or posthypnotically? To test this possibility, Brady and Rosner (1966) gave suggestions to subjects under hypnosis to experience a dream. It was noticed shortly thereafter that REM activity was present in these subjects. This would indicate a general similarity between dreams produced during real sleep and dreams induced during hypnosis. However, Evans, Reich, and Orne (1972) tried to replicate the Brady and Rosner study with better controls to minimize the possibility that subjects in the previous study produced their results as a function of demand characteristics. These investigators failed to find REM during hypnotically induced dreams. Thus, it would appear that further research is essential to determine if, in fact, REM can be produced during hypnotically induced dream states.

In summary, there appears to be no substantial evidence to indicate that the processes responsible for sleep-type dreams are related to hypnotically induced dreams. However, much more research is necessary on this topic before any conclusive statement can be made that they are totally independent of each other.

Even if the relationship between hypnosis, sleep and dreams is marginal at best, it is possible that hypnosis can be used to alter sleep or sleep cycles. For instance, Tart (1970) found that direct, hypnotic suggestions could be used to awaken subjects from normal sleep at a predetermined and suggested time. Two additional studies (Halper, Pivik, and Dement, 1969; Stoyva, 1965) also have investigated the effects of hypnosis on sleep.

Halper, Pivik, and Dement (1969) investigated dreaming behavior during sleep. Since dreaming typically occurs during REM phases of sleep, and if such dreaming is not allowed to occur (by waking the subject during REM phases) over a series of sleep sessions, a recovery period may follow: that is, when the subject subsequently is allowed to sleep normally, without interruption, a greater than normal amount of REM sleep ensues. Halper, Pivik, and Dement were interested in determining if hypnotically induced dreaming could substitute for "lost" REM sleep and consequent sleep dreaming. To investigate this possibility, subjects who had been found to be highly hypnotizable were allowed to sleep in a normal fashion. When REM sleep occurred, the subjects were awakened. For three consecutive nights, these subjects were not permitted to experience REM sleep and consequent dreams. Using hypnosis, Halper, Pivik, and Dement induced dreaming behavior and hypnotic hallucinations. They found that hypnotically induced dreaming did not substitute for REM sleep dreaming. The recovery phenomenon of making up for lost REM sleep still occurred regardless of the induction and substitution of hypnosis-type dreams.

Also related to dreams and sleep, Stoyva (1965) considered the possible influence of hypnosis via posthypnotic suggestion on specific dream content during REM sleep. Suggesting to subjects that certain events or objects would be part of their sleep dreams, he found that many subjects did experience dreams that were influenced by his hypnotic suggestions. It appears that hypnosis can be used to influence dream content for some subjects.

A fascinating subtopic of hypnosis and sleep is the presumed ability of some subjects to learn algebra or a foreign language, for instance, while asleep. Reports published in popular magazines have speculated that learning during sleep may be a possibility. Can this learning be accomplished?

After a series of experiments indicating that learning during sleep was possible, Simon and Emmons (1956) showed that, for the most part, the ability to perform this feat was far exaggerated. They found that information presented for learning purposes during "sleep" was recalled only when alpha brain activity had occurred during presentation of the material. Since alpha activity generally is not associated with a state of sleep, but rather with a state of wakefulness, they felt that any learning that occurred was the result of learning during a waking state.

However, since dream content can be influenced in subjects highly susceptible to hypnosis, is it possible that such subjects also could learn to acquire nondream information during sleep? In other words, although Simon and Emmons found a general lack of the ability to learn during sleep, they may have failed to consider susceptibility to suggestions in or out of a state of sleep as an influencing factor. It may be possible that subjects highly susceptible to hypnotic suggestion also may be highly susceptible to suggestions to learn information during sleep. This possibility was considered by Evans (1972).

In that study, subjects high or low in hypnotic susceptibility were selected who could respond to sleep-administered suggestion: that is, these subjects showed signs of the ability to follow suggestions that could influence dream content or other behavior (e.g., "you are feeling cold"—the subject responds by pulling a blanket over his body). Also, as a result of Simon and Emmons' findings, information presented during alpha brain activity was not counted as learning information. In addition, all subjects received a strong and motivated waking set that sleep learning was possible. The results of Evans' study clearly indicated that some material presented during sleep was recalled upon awakening, particularly by subjects who were prejudged to be highly susceptible to hypnotic suggestion and who were found to recall the greatest amount of information. It appears, therefore, that sleep learning for some subjects is possible under optimal laboratory conditions. While it is not known whether subjects judged highly susceptible to hypnosis can listen to recorded information while asleep and recall some of it upon waking, the experimental evidence would indicate that this might be a fairly strong possibility.

Hypnosis and ESP

With regard to the ability to learn information presented during sleep, some individuals claim (with some experimental support) that they can "pick up" sources of information presented far from their present location during sleep or during a waking state; namely, some individuals appear to possess an extrasensory ability to process information. This area of research has received a considerable amount of attention. In addition, some investigators have considered the relationship between hypnosis and the ability to experience extrasensory perception or ESP. Specifically, can hypnotic suggestions facilitate ESP performance? Honorton and Krippner (1969) have reviewed the research in this area, examining some rather interesting reports and conclusions. Some of the experiments they cite include those by Grela (1945), Fahler and Cadoret (1958), and Casler (1962, 1967).

Grela undertook the first systematic investigation of the effects of hypnosis on ESP performance. Two groups of subjects were employed. One group was judged as being high in hypnotic susceptibility, the second group, low. The task of the experiment was to guess symbols displayed on a deck of cards not visible to the subjects. Subjects high in hypnotic susceptibility received suggestions under hypnosis that they possessed ESP abilities and that these abilities would be displayed more than adequately when they were asked to guess symbols appearing on hidden cards. Subjects low in hypnotic susceptibility received similar instructions, but no hypnosis was employed. Although Grela's results did not prove to be statistically significant, a trend was exhibited: hypnosis tended to facilitate card-guessing accuracy.

In a related study by Fahler and Cadoret (1958), subjects high in hypnotic susceptibility participated in an ESP experiment during a waking state, as well as during a state of hypnosis. During the waking state, when the assignment was to guess symbols on cards in a fashion similar to that employed by Grela, the number of correct guesses did not exceed chance. However, in the hypnotized state a very high level of performance was achieved, far exceeding chance.

Casler (1962, 1967) also found that subjects demonstrated ESP abilities significantly better with hypnotic facilitation than during a waking state. In the latter study, subjects were asked to generate during hypnosis whatever suggestions of their own they felt would help them perform better in an ESP task. As with the previous technique in which the experimenter induced hypnotic suggestions of enhanced ESP abilities, self-induced suggestion during hypnosis was found to be effective in producing improved guessing ability in an ESP task.

Additional possible facilitating effects of hypnosis on ESP abilities have been tested by Rhine (1946). Rhine was interested in determining if psychokinetic abilities could be facilitated with hypnosis so that a subject could influence the outcome of a throw of dice. Although the results were in the affirmative direction, hypnosis did not appear to have a marked effect on psychokinesis.

Krippner (1968) reported a study concerned with the effects of hypnotic imagery on ESP performance. When subjects were instructed to concentrate on an image that they could not physically see but which the experimenter could, Krippner found that hypnotized subjects were better able to accurately report the content of the image. He concluded that hypnosis may have served to "speed up" the processing of extrasensory material.

Clairvoyant dreams also have been studied as a result of hypnotic susceptibility and subsequent hypnotizability (Honorton and Stump, 1969; Honorton, 1972). In the former study, subjects judged high in hypnotic susceptibility were given suggestions to dream while under hypnosis. They were told to dream about the contents of an envelope. Specifically, the task of the experiment was to visualize via imagery, if possible, an object contained in a closed envelope. The results of the Honorton and Stump study, for the most part, did not indicate the ability of subjects to use clairvoyant dreams to assist them in this task. In a more controlled study (Honorton, 1972), however, it was reported that content guessing was significantly improved in subjects experiencing clairvoyant dreams under hypnosis. Thus, although the evidence is far from conclusive, it appears that clairvoyant dreams induced under hypnosis may facilitate, to a degree, ESP abilities for some subjects.

Because the previously cited studies appear to indicate the facilitation of some ESP abilities under hypnosis, one might ask if the subjects employed in such studies already possessed some of these abilities. For the most part, it appears from the description of studies cited that no effort was made to determine if subjects did or did not possess such ESP abilities. However, many of the studies did test subjects under many conditions including a waking state as well as a hypnotic state. Only with the latter state did even an approximation to a facilitative effect of ESP abilities occur. Therefore, this seemingly obvious control may not have been that crucial. Something more important, however, may have been the presence of demand characteristics or the ability to deduce the desired outcome of experiments. This could have influenced results to a degree. Also, the presentation order of various conditions was not always controlled. For instance, if a hypnosis condition always followed a waking condition, one could not be certain if hypnosis influenced the outcome of the experiment or if the presentation order of conditions was the contributing factor. Before it can be stated conclusively that hypnosis facilitates ESP abilities, greater and more precise experimental control must be imposed.

If necessary experimental controls were to be imposed on ESP experiments, would it be possible to judge whether ESP abilities could be improved in a manner similar to the training of hypnotizability as described in chapter 2? There is some evidence to indicate that this may be a possibility with the use of hypnosis (Ryzl, 1962, 1966).

Ryzl divides his training technique into three parts. The first part consists of extensively training the subject in hypnosis, so that he becomes able to experience very vivid visual imagery through hypnotically induced hallucinations. After this has been accomplished and while the subject still is in a state of hypnosis, he is given some simple tasks to perform. These may include having the subject, with his eyes closed, identify objects placed in front of him. If he is capable of identifying some of these objects, the experimenter then tries to increase the subject's ability. This usually takes the form of having the subject continuously produce visual imagery of increasingly complicated and difficult identifications. In this manner, the subject is also "taught" to distinguish reliable hallucinations from false ones. Exactly how this process functions Ryzl does not specify, but he does state that it helps reduce the subject's error rate. The final training stage consists of gradually reducing the subject's dependence upon the experimenter, and reducing and eventually eliminating the use of hypnosis to produce the visual imagery or clairvoyant dreams (hallucinations). Ryzl claims that with this training technique involving hypnosis, 10 percent of his subjects showed improved ESP abilities.

Obviously, Ryzl's technique is very controversial. As he does not specify the baseline ESP performance of his subjects, magnitude of improvement in determining ESP abilities as a function of training is not possible. However, as Ryzl's technique has received some experimental support (Ryzl and Ryzlova, 1962; Beloff and Mandelberg, 1966), it may be assumed to be of some value. Before an accurate assessment of this technique can be made, more carefully controlled laboratory experiments are necessary.

With regard to ESP performance and hypnosis, it appears that hypnosis facilitates such performance through enhancing the subject's ability to produce veridical visual imagery. However, why this is the case or how the process functions behaviorally and physiologically is not known. Unless the mystical and magical quality of ESP research is removed and the phenomenon treated in a more rigorous and scientific manner with adequate theoretical explanations of results, it always will remain a controversial area of research. In fact, contemporary ESP research appears to be in the stage of development approximating the Mesmerian era of hypnosis research and study. It is hoped that in the future this state of affairs will improve.

9

Stage Hypnosis

FOR MANY YEARS hypnosis has been used as a medium of entertainment. Although one might question the ethics of doing so, hypnosis often is used on stage in demonstrations of phenomena intended to make the layperson view them as extraordinary feats of power and magic. Individuals who bill themselves as stage hypnotists usually are not practitioners of applied hypnosis in any of the areas previously described. They often do not possess the necessary educational credentials such as a degree in one of the professional fields employing hypnosis. More important is the fact that they use hypnosis neither to help cure, nor investigate, but merely to entertain.

When a stage hypnotist performs hypnosis before an audience, why does it appear that he induces a hypnotic state so easily? Just as the surgeon, dentist, or psychologist employing hypnosis must determine the level of hypnotic susceptibility of his subject, this is also the case with a stage hypnotist *prior to* his live, stage performance. Before performing his act, the stage hypnotist often will ask for a group of volunteers from his audience. Since these individuals have volunteered, it is assumed that they have the positive attitudes, motivation, and expectancies to be willing to take suggestions from a hypnotist (Barber, Spanos, and Chaves, 1974). However, since the volunteer pool often consists of far too many subjects, it is necessary to eliminate some of them. Naturally, the hypnotist does not wish to eliminate subjects highly susceptible to hypnosis. Therefore, he will ask all of the volunteers to perform a series of tasks backstage and will choose those who best perform the tasks. These tasks are simply hypnotic susceptibility tests, discussed previously in chapter 2. Just as the Stanford or Harvard hypnotic tasks range from easy to hard-to-perform, so also does the series of tasks that the stage hypnotist asks his subjects to perform. The first screening procedure is designed to eliminate those subjects deemed low in hypnotic susceptibility or hard to hypnotize. For this procedure, the hypnotist may ask his subjects to perform one of the easiest tasks, either from one of the standardized scales discussed in chapter 2, or a task analogous to one of the first levels of the scales. Such a task may be one of arm lowering, one involving the postural sway, or one concerned with eye closure.

Before administering one of the aforementioned tests of susceptibility, all subjects usually are asked to be seated on chairs or on the floor. The hypnotist then introduces himself to his volunteers and thanks them for volunteering. He explains to them that he cannot possibly use all of them in his demonstrations and that he must use those who are deemed most readily hypnotizable and cooperative. His introductory comments set the stage for his volunteers in terms of future expectations. Since subjects are hypnotized more readily if they are led to believe that the situation involves hypnosis and is defined as hypnosis (Barber and Calverley, 1964, 1965), it is important that the performer introduce himself as a hypnotist. Also, as only some of the volunteers will be selected to be hypnotized on stage, the hypnotist wishes to use those most highly motivated to be cooperative with hypnotic suggestion. Thus, explaining to the group that only a few of them will be used for demonstrations of hypnotic tasks on stage will increase the motivation of the entire group of volunteers to perform as well as they can during the screening procedures.

After the introductory preliminaries, the hypnotist will commence with a simple hypnotic susceptibility screening test such as arm lowering. In brief, this task involves the ability of a subject to lower his arm from a horizontal, rigid position at the suggestion of the hypnotist. Using this test, the hypnotist is able to screen the performance of the volunteers and to determine which subjects have or have not complied with his arm lowering suggestion. Those who have failed to perform this simple task adequately are politely asked to return to their seats among the nonvolunteer audience. As many of the volunteers will have performed this task adequately, more difficult screening tests subsequently are employed. These may include the hand clasp and/or eye catalepsy (see chapter 2). After subjects are asked to perform one or both of these tasks, further screening takes place. Such screening procedures continue until the stage hypnotist has selected the most highly susceptible and cooperative subjects.

The aforementioned screening procedure is one of several principles enumerated by Meeker and Barber (1971) which underlie stage hypnosis. Another principle is the knowledge that the base level or "waking" responsiveness to suggestions is much higher than is commonly assumed. In essence, the so-called hypnotic trance which an audience believes is necessary for hypnosis, in fact, is unnecessary for a large portion of volunteers if they are high in hypnotic susceptibility (Anderson and Sarbin, 1964; Barber, 1969).

Stage hypnotists also define the situation as hypnosis. When this is the case, it becomes fairly clear to subjects that a high level of responsiveness to suggestions and to commands is desired and expected.

Another stage hypnosis principle is the notion that a stage setting for a performance has unique expectancy characteristics which are very helpful in eliciting apparent hypnotic behavior. As Orne (1962) has noted, subjects watching a performance do not believe that they would do some of the things they observe others doing on stage. However, when they are on stage, they do, in fact, seldom refuse to play the stage participant role. Thus, the stage hypnotist has a considerable amount of social-psychological control over his subjects.

Many stage hypnotists also rely on the use of so-called stage whispers. This involves the whispering of private instructions to the subject that help make the stage demonstration successful. The subject is asked to cooperate in doing what he is asked to do to help make the performance a success even if hypnosis does not take place.

The failure to challenge subjects with regard to the presence of hypnosis is also a common principle of stage hypnosis: that is, when a hypnotic suggestion is given to a subject, the hypnotist does not challenge him to determine whether or not the suggestion was effective. For instance, if arm rigidity is being demonstrated, the hypnotist may not challenge the subject to try to bend his arm. Therefore, the hypnotist and the audience really do not know if the suggestion actually was effective. Instead, they presume that hypnosis took place. Whether it did or not is relatively unimportant to a successful performance if the subject is cooperative.

Many stage hypnotists also employ stooges or pretrained subjects to ensure the success of their demonstrations. When the hypnotist asks for volunteers from the audience, he may choose collaborators, not true volunteers. Such stooges often were used to demonstrate the more difficult feats in which a high level of hypnotic susceptibility is necessary. However, this was primarily a practice during the vaudeville era; the use of stooges by stage hypnotists today is rather rare.

A good stage hypnotist often will use one or more tricks to elicit unusual behavior from his volunteers. They are necessary for a successful, entertaining performance by the stage hypnotist. Some of these tricks are enumerated by Meeker and Barber (1971).

One of the most common tricks is referred to as the human plank feat. This involves the ability of a subject to maintain a rigid posture in a horizontal position between two chairs. The demonstration of this task commences with the hypnotist suggesting to the subject that his body will be absolutely rigid. This suggestion usually is given while the hypnotist looks the subject in the eye and puts him into a "hypnotic trance." This episode may be followed by a suggested postural sway, the subject being asked to fall backward in a rigid position. The hypnotist and an assistant or two catch the subject before he falls, lift him, and place him between two chairs. The audience then observes that the subject remains completely stiff and rigid between the chairs. This feat usually brings a loud round of applause from the audience. After the applause the hypnotist may ask his assistant to stand on the chest of the volunteer who is maintaining the rigid posture. This is accomplished and is followed by another round of applause. The hypnotist then asks the assistant to step down off the volunteer's chest. The volunteer is removed from between the two chairs and stood up in a vertical position. Then he is given a suggestion of feeling normal and nonrigid. The subject looks about the audience at this point and a loud round of applause follows.

How does the stage hypnotist perform this feat so well and easily? The answer is simply that the stage hypnotist relies on several nonhypnotic phenomena usually not familiar to an audience. For instance, very few individuals realize that if a subject is placed between two chairs, one below his head and the other at his ankles, he usually can easily maintain balance in this position *without* any hypnotic suggestion whatsoever. Barber (1969) found that 80 percent of a group of unselected subjects (i.e., level of hypnotic susceptibility not determined) were able to maintain suspension between two chairs when they were told simply to keep their bodies rigid. Also, subjects in such a position can fairly easily maintain the weight of another person if the weight is applied to the chest area. Consequently, the human plank feat can be performed easily without hypnosis if one places the two chairs in the appropriate locations.

Another trick commonly employed by stage hypnotists, known as eyeball fastening, requires a subject to close his eyes and to roll his eyeballs upward as far as possible. After the subject is told continuously to keep his eyelids closed tight while looking higher and higher toward his forehead, he is challenged to open his eyes. When the subject is unable to do so, the expected applause arises from the audience. This feat also is easy to explain. If one attempts to open his eyes while his eyeballs are rolled upward, he finds that it is physically impossible to do so. As a result, almost anyone could perform this feat.

Hypnotic anesthesia is another commonly employed stage feat. It is used to demonstrate that a subject can be anesthetized sufficiently with the aid of hypnosis so that he experiences no pain when a needle or another sharp object is applied to a limb, usually an arm. In performing this feat the hypnotist asks the subject to extend an arm horizontally with the palm facing downward. The stage hypnotist then suggests numbness and the absence of all sensations in the limb, in a manner similar to that described in chapter 4. Briefly, the subject is instructed that sensations he normally experiences will leave his arm, and that his arm will feel as if it had received a massive dose of novocaine. As the anesthesia instructions continue, the hypnotist may take a long, sterilized hat pin and run it through the subject's arm. To the amazement of the audience the subject shows no overt signs of experiencing any pain. Therefore, they assume, his arm must have been hypnotically anesthetized.

Another common feat is to run a hot object along the subject's palm and finger area to demonstrate the effects of hypnotic anesthesia for the elimination of experienced pain. As all viewers from the audience realize that the application of heat to skin hurts, they observe in awe the absence of pain sensations on the part of the participant as a hot object is run from his palm area to his fingers and back.

These two demonstrations of the absence of pain can be produced easily with the use of hypnotic anesthesia. The procedures and applications of hypnotic anesthesia were described in chapter 4. However, such anesthesia really is not necessary in the demonstration of the alleviation or reduction of pain. In the pin injection demonstration, if the hypnotist does not inform the subject that such an object will be applied to his skin, a very cooperative subject will appear to experience no pain. In addition, if the hypnotist pinches the area of the arm in which he is injecting the sharp instrument, very little, if any, pain is experienced. Thus, although hypnotic anesthesia easily can be used to alleviate pain during the performance of the pin injection feat, it really is not necessary in the performance of the trick.

The explanation of the heat trick is also quite simple.

Again, although hypnotic anesthesia can eliminate the experienced feelings of pain when, for instance, a match or cigarette lighter flame is passed under a subject's palm, the phenomenon has a nonhypnotic explanation. Tracy (1952) has demonstrated that if a flame is held about one inch from a subject's palm, anyone (high or low in hypnotic susceptibility) easily can withstand the pain provided that the flame is kept moving at a steady pace.

Blood flow stoppage is a stage feat also employed by many hypnotists. In demonstrating this phenomenon, the hypnotist can use a stooge or a volunteer subject. When a stooge is used, the phenomenon can be produced by two different means (Meeker and Barber, 1971). One method requires a stooge to sit on a chair for a period of time in such a fashion (not perceptible to the audience, of course) as to cut off the circulation of blood to one arm. When he is asked to stand, the audience easily can see that one arm (the one the stooge pressed against the chair) is pale white, while the other arm is normal and flesh colored. This method of stopping the flow of blood can be demonstrated easily. The reader may even recall awaking some mornings without sensation in a given limb. The limb feels totally numb or tingly. In fact, the flow of blood to that limb has been cut off in the same manner in which the stooge stopped the flow of blood to his arm. This happened as a result of sleeping in a position that inhibited the normal blood flow to a given limb. After a few minutes, of course, the blood flow is reestablished and "life" returns to the limb.

A second method of producing the blood flow stoppage feat is to have a stooge hold a golf ball or other similar object far up under one of his arms. This procedure also stops the normal flow of blood to the arm when the stooge presses against the ball. This technique reduces possible suspicions from the audience that a chair was instrumental in producing the blood flow stoppage.

A third method has been described by Meeker and Barber (1971) that can be used with normal, volunteer subjects, rather than stooges. In this method the subject is asked to clench his fist with his arm at his side. The stage hypnotist then suggests to the subject that his arm is becoming very rigid and that the

blood flow that normally occurs in his arm will be altered so
that it will flow out of his arm. The hypnotist then will take
hold of the subject's arm and swing it upward to a horizontal
position while continuing to give suggestions of rigidity in the
arm. The result of this procedure is to produce a cramp in the
muscles of the arm. This produces the effect of a pale white
arm and the hypnotist explains to the audience that the "blood
has left the subject's arm."

Another feat commonly employed in stage hypnosis is
demonstrating the power of the hypnotist to make the subject
go limp and fall asleep instantly through the use of hypnosis.
In this phenomenon the hypnotist always will apply his hands
to the subject's head while giving him a series of suggestions
with the following included: "You are going completely limp.
You will be totally under my powers and will fall completely
asleep when I tell you to do so." The audience then observes
carefully as the subject does "fall asleep" on the spot. As with
all the previously described stage hypnosis phenomena, this
trick has a simple explanation.

When performing the "instant sleep" feat, the stage hypnotist puts his hands on the subject's face and exerts pressure
on the baroreceptors at the carotid sinus. This produces a
vagus-induced bradycardia (relatively slow heart action) and
vasodilation (widening of the hollow of blood vessels) which
leads to sudden hypotension (abnormally low blood pressure)
and fainting (Ganong, 1967). This technique is potentially
dangerous, especially if used on subjects suffering from high
blood pressure or heart disease. For such individuals, brain
damage or even death could result primarily from a lack of
blood if the carotid pressure is maintained for too long. As a
result, fifteen seconds is considered to be the maximum safe level
for performing this trick (Whitlow, 1948).

In addition to the stage feats enumerated by Meeker and
Barber (1971), many performing hypnotists will demonstrate
phenomena more legitimately classified as hypnosis. One such
phenomenon is a posthypnotic suggestion. In chapter 2, in the
description of the Harvard Group Scale of Hypnotic Susceptibility, it will be recalled that one of the more difficult subtests
of hypnotic susceptibility was concerned with the reaching for

an ankle upon hearing a precipitating stimulus such as a tapping noise initiated by the hypnotist. When questioned about his behavior, the subject does not know why he reached for his ankle, because the act involved a posthypnotic suggestion. During hypnosis the subject had been instructed that upon hearing a tapping sound after returning to a normal state of consciousness, he automatically and freely would reach for his right or left ankle. Such posthypnotic suggestions often are employed in stage hypnosis because they can be quite entertaining. The stage demonstration possibilities with posthypnotic suggestions are inexhaustible. For example, stage hypnotists may ask subjects to perform a variety of acts and "feats" posthypnotically, such as singing the "Star-Spangled Banner" after seeing the hypnotist reach for his right ear, or throwing a tantrum on the stage floor after hearing the hypnotist call his name. In performing this type of an act for his audience, the hypnotist has at his disposal an endless variety of potentially entertaining acts. When an audience observes a hypnosis volunteer make a fool of himself in the performance of some unusual act on stage, it probably is the result of a posthypnotic suggestion. Often the subject also is given the suggestion that he will not remember being given the posthypnotic instruction or know why he is performing the act. This hypnotic amnesia adds to the entertainment value of the stage performance and generally enhances the credibility of the stage hypnotist for the audience as a man of "many powers." Of course, he really is not omnipotent. He simply is using for entertainment purposes well-established phenomena used in hypnotic therapeutic situations (see chapter 3). The psychologist employing hypnotherapy often will use posthypnotic suggestions and hypnotic amnesia in the treatment of phobias or other behavioral problems.

Hypnotic hallucinations also are used by some stage hypnotists. Just as some subjects highly susceptible to hypnosis are able to perceive the presence of an imaginary fly in one of the subtests of the Harvard hypnotic scale, many volunteer participants in stage hypnosis can be made to see things which are not physically present (called positive hallucinations) or can be made not to see objects which are present (called negative hallucinations). For example, a hypnotist can suggest to a subject that it is raining on stage. The audience laughs as the subject heads for cover to protect himself from the deluge. Another commonly employed positive hallucination is concerned with experienced temperature. For example, a subject can be told that the room temperature is becoming extremely hot when, in fact, it is very cold. The audience watches as the subject perspires profusely and perhaps removes articles of clothing. This demonstration often receives a round of loud applause and considerable laughter. The number of positive hallucinations that can be invented for stage hypnosis demonstrations is limited only by the hypnotist's imagination.

A negative hallucination feat commonly performed in stage hypnosis includes the "observation" by the subject of a cigarette hanging in midair. This feat is accomplished by suggesting to the subject that the hypnotist will become invisible when he lights a cigarette. The subject then observes in amazement what he perceives to be a lit cigarette hanging in the air. In the negative hallucination suggestion, the hypnotist "disappears" from the subject's sight, a phenomenon that is contingent upon the posthypnotic suggestion of observing the hypnotist light a cigarette. As with positive hallucinations, the hypnotist can devise a variety of negative hallucinations to perform before an audience.

A great deal of the hypnotist's success is based upon his ability to be a good entertainer as well as to know the basics of hypnosis and its induction procedures. Brandon (1956) gives a few additional pointers for a successful performance with stage hypnotism. She believes that the real secret to successful stage hypnotism lies in the performer's skill in arousing the undivided attention of the audience and focusing such attention directly upon the subject being hypnotized. Once such attention is achieved, it can be maintained and held throughout the performance by a successful hypnotist. This, of course, requires the development of a good repertoire of feats to be performed by subjects. Brandon also emphasizes that a good stage hypnotist maintains a poised appearance, a friendly smile, and a gaze steadily directed into the eyes of the audience, not above their heads. In addition, the type of clothing worn by the hypnotist during a performance is important. The hypnotist who is most successful in maintaining the interest of his audience usually wears semi-formal clothing that is not so fancy in appearance that it distracts the attention from the hypnosis performance.

One problem which inevitably arises in a discussion of stage hypnosis is the issue of ethics. Is it ethical for a nontherapist to practice hypnosis, and before an audience, for nontherapeutic means? Professionals (psychologists, physicians), for the most part, consider the use of hypnosis outside a therapeutic setting to be unethical. As a matter of fact, professional hypnosis societies, such as the Society of Clinical and Experimental Hypnosis, frown upon the idea of anyone practicing hypnosis without both a doctorate earned from an accredited university and practical experience in the use of hypnosis. It goes without saying that the majority of stage hypnotists do not possess these credentials. Therefore, in a sense, they are being unethical in the use of hypnosis for entertainment purposes. However, there is no law in any of the fifty states expressly forbidding the use and/or demonstration of hypnosis and hypnotic phenomena. Thus, even though professionals frown upon the use of stage hypnosis, they are totally powerless to put a stop to such performances. In addition, as there is little, if any, psychological or personal danger inherent in the demonstrations involved in stage hypnosis, the entire ethical and legal concerns of many persons may be somewhat exaggerated.

Stage hypnosis is entertaining and such demonstrations usually draw large audiences. Although this form of hypnosis does not have an application except to entertain, it has served the purpose of popularizing hypnosis and making many individuals aware of its uses, as well as abuses. Thus, individuals may discover through a stage performance of hypnosis that there are possible beneficial uses of hypnotism. As a result, they eventually may consider hypnotherapy as a possible means of treating, with the aid of a specialist, a behavioral problem or disorder. If this were to occur, it would appear that stage hypnosis could play a valuable role in promoting the use of hypnosis in professional settings.

On the other hand, some persons have been discouraged from considering professional hypnotherapy because of the magical, mystical quality often incorporated into stage hypnosis by some performers. As a result of the many myths and half-truths perpetuated through stage hypnosis, problems often are created for professional hypnotherapists. Frequently, it is necessary for them to spend many hours with patients/clients exposing some of the trickery of stage hypnosis and detailing the true nature of hypnosis and hypnotic suggestions.

The controversy concerning the ethical and legal aspects of stage hypnosis will undoubtedly continue. Obviously, it can be beneficial as well as detrimental in furthering the use of therapeutically applied hypnosis in today's society.

10

The Future of Hypnosis

MANY APPLIED USES of hypnosis have been described in the chapters of this book. They include the treatment of behavioral disorders—phobias, obsessions, compulsions, and anxiety—and the treatment of unwanted habits—overeating and smoking. The use of hypnosis as an anesthetic, an analgesic, and as a useful instrument in the treatment of various sexual dysfunctions also has been examined.

Now we may ask, what is the future of hypnosis? What beneficial aspects of hypnosis have, as yet, been untapped? If hypnosis is to be used more frequently for various treatments in the future, what will be the ramifications in terms of ethical considerations? Will legal restrictions be placed upon the use of hypnosis and upon those who may use it?

Future uses of hypnosis will be determined as much by the imagination as the future uses of any therapy or manipulation. However, Fromm (1972) conducted a survey of many researchers in the field of hypnosis and asked them to indicate their future, proposed, or in-progress hypnosis endeavors. Some rather interesting results were obtained from the respondents. To summarize Fromm's findings, the future research areas of hypnosis basically will expand upon present uses of this manipulation. However, some unique projects also were delineated. For example, several researchers expressed interest in examining the phenomenon of self-hypnosis and its increased use in future therapies. Unfortunately, the time, effort, and expense involved in seeing a hypnotherapist for a given problem prevent many individuals from seeking this treatment. Also, many physicians, dentists, and other potential users of hypnotic techniques generally have shied away from adopting such techniques because in their judgment it is too expensive and time-consuming. The solution requires some procedure by which individuals can be taught to hypnotize themselves before treatment for a given disorder. In this fashion the great amount of time usually spent by a hypnotherapist in hypnotizing his patient could be saved.

As ideal as self-hypnosis sounds, however, it still is necessary for a potential patient to be tested for hypnotic susceptibility and to be hypnotized at least once by the therapist before self-hypnosis can be employed. These procedures obviously are necessary to determine if the patient can profit by hypnosis and to allow him to experience the phenomenon. Only after this is accomplished satisfactorily can the patient be taught self-hypnosis for future use.

Self-hypnosis could be employed beneficially by patients suffering from such problems as anxiety attacks or from chronic pain resulting from arthritis, rheumatism, or cancer. It must be cautioned, however, that self-hypnosis for the reduction of pain in these afflictions should never be thought of as a substitute for chemotherapy. It can be used only as an adjunct, to allow for reduced doses of an administered drug. In addition, if chronic pain is severe, self-hypnosis will be much more difficult for the patient to achieve, and assistance still may be necessary from a qualified professional trained in the methods and techniques of hypnosis or from a family member trained in hypnotic techniques by a professional.

However, even with the limitations of self-hypnosis, the future trends of hypnotherapy would indicate an increasing reliance on this technique in treatments. If both the patient and the therapist can save time and money by its adoption, its use for treatment may increase where hypnosis is deemed to be potentially beneficial.

Another trend in the future use of hypnosis, according to Fromm, may be the increased use of hypnotherapy in group settings. Traditionally, hypnotherapy has been conducted on a one-to-one basis. However, as was mentioned, this procedure can be expensive as well as time-consuming. Therefore, some researchers, as well as practicing clinical psychologists, are experimenting with the administration of treatment via hypnosis to groups of individuals. This obviously is a time-saver for the professional, since many patients can be treated simultaneously. This approach would be likely to work well for simple habit-control problems such as smoking and/or overeating. In this manner a group of smokers or overeaters could all be treated in a common session. This approach already has been used extensively by Garrett (1972) with reported success.

Although hypnotherapy has been applied to the control and treatment of smoking and overeating, very little contemporary research has focused on the potential use of hypnosis in the treatment of drug addiction. Future trends of hypnosis research may move in this direction. Hypnosis may be able to help control the amount of drug intake or to substitute hypnotically-induced sensations for drug-produced sensations. The use of hypnosis with drug addicts, as well as with alcoholics, may allow for a new therapy to be used in conjunction with existing treatment methods or, possibly, to be used by itself as a substitute for sensations produced by drugs. In this manner hypnosis could be used to produce a safe hallucination or "high."

Another major area of future research in hypnosis, according to Fromm, will be in identifying personality characteristics or correlates of hypnotizability. Chapter 2 mentioned several of these correlates. Future research endeavors undoubtedly will identify more variables that contribute to or are related to the ability of an individual to be readily hypnotized. The importance of identifying such variables cannot be overstressed. Eventually, the identification of strong correlates of hypnotizability may allow for the use of this information as a rapid screening procedure in identifying those who will profit most from hypnosis in a given therapy and when they will profit most. Ultimately, simple procedures might be established for faster (and, thus, less expensive) screening of subjects for determining the level of hypnotizability for treatment with hypnotherapy.

The future of hypnosis also will depend on developments in the medical profession. The increase in malpractice suits against physicians and anesthesiologists increases the possibility that whenever chemical anesthesia might be less safe for some patients than for others, a greater reliance might be placed on the extremely safe method of administering an anesthetic effect via hypnotic suggestion.

Also, with regard to the topic of malpractice, the future uses of hypnosis might be restricted to applied settings such as psychology clinics and medical facilities. Although hypnosis, per se, is not dangerous, many professional or pseudo-professional practitioners of hypnosis often promise more than they can deliver, yet charge handsomely for their services, regardless of results. Many who seek treatment do not receive satisfactory results. Whether or not this is the fault of the therapist, it could contribute to a malpractice suit. To avoid such potential suits many hypnotherapists, like physicians, will be conservative in their treatment procedures and in promised or anticipated results. In addition, the threat of potential malpractice suits may produce tighter ethical controls in terms of when and by whom hypnosis is to be used.

Despite the restrictions that may be imposed upon its use, the future of applied hypnosis looks fairly bright. More and more applications of hypnosis may be seen in medical, behavioral, and allied fields in future years to the benefit of mankind and society.

One area in which hypnosis could be beneficial is education. For instance, it might be used to help some children concentrate better or learn faster, especially if problems exist in these areas. However, until the mystical element of hypnosis is removed, it is unlikely that parents, teachers, or administrators will permit its wide usage.

Clearly, the future of hypnosis will depend not only upon scientific research and expanded applications but also upon a good public relations campaign designed to eliminate the sensationalized half-truths, inaccuracies and existing mystical elements that surround the term hypnosis. It is hoped that this was partially accomplished by this book, because an accurate picture of hypnosis is vital to its future. The full beneficial and widespread use of hypnosis cannot become a reality until it is recognized as an extremely useful and legitimate tool in the treatment of many disorders.

Appendix

Self-Rating Hypnotic Susceptibility Scale

THE FOLLOWING SCALE permits you to assess your own level of hypnotic susceptibility. This test is to be taken *by yourself* in a quiet, preferably semi-dark environment undisturbed by any distractions. Eight tasks are to be performed in assessing your score. For each task you are able to satisfactorily complete, give yourself one point. Please follow the instructions as closely as possible and perform the tasks in order.

You may find it easiest to administer this test to yourself if you record the tasks and instructions on tape and listen to them in the previously described environment. Furthermore, compliance with hypnotic suggestions is best achieved when you are as relaxed as possible. If you are not in a relaxed state, try isolating yourself in a dark, quiet environment for at least fifteen minutes before administering this test.

1. *Sustained Stare*. Select any object in a room and stare at it for approximately five minutes. If you are capable of main-

taining such a stare without interruption for the required
period of time, give yourself one point.

2. *Eye Closure.* Make yourself as relaxed as possible by sitting
   still with your eyes closed for a few minutes. Then instruct
   yourself to open your eyes. Tell yourself that your eyelids are
   becoming very, very heavy. Continue giving yourself this
   suggestion until you feel your eyelids closing. If your eyelids do close, give yourself one point.

3. *Finger Lock.* Again make yourself as relaxed as possible.
   Now interlock the fingers of both hands. Tell yourself that
   your fingers are becoming bound together tighter and
   tighter. Continue giving yourself this suggestion for about
   two minutes. Following this period of time, try as hard as
   you can to pull your hands apart. A failure to separate your
   hands after about fifteen seconds of trying indicates that you
   have performed adequately and you should give yourself one
   point.

4. *Arm Rigidity.* Extend one of your arms directly in front of
   you. Tell yourself over and over again that your arm is becoming very, very rigid—as stiff as a metal pipe. Following
   about two minutes of this suggestion, try to bend your arm.
   If it does not immediately and readily bend, give yourself one
   point.

5. *Arm Levitation.* As in the previous task, extend your arm.
   Tell yourself that your arm is becoming very, very light—as
   light as a feather. Say that it feels as if it is so light that it is
   able to defy gravity and will rise like a hot-air balloon. If
   your arm does rise, give yourself one point.

6. *Hand Movement.* Position your hands with the palms
   facing one another. Tell yourself that a force exists between
   your hands that prevents them from moving toward one
   another. Say that it feels as if your hands are like the
   repelling sides of two magnets, prevented from touching
   each other. If a struggle ensues and your hands do not touch
   for at least thirty seconds, give yourself one point.

7. *Itch Suggestion.* Make yourself very, very relaxed. Now
   begin thinking about an itching sensation on your right ear
   lobe. Tell yourself over and over again that it feels very, very
   tingly and irritated. Say that you cannot help but scratch to

relieve this itch. If you begin to scratch your ear lobe after about two minutes of continuous suggestion, give yourself one point.

8. *Imagination.* While in a very, very relaxed state, imagine the presence of any object or person of your choosing. Try as hard as you can to produce a vivid image of this object or person in intense color, as if you were watching it on the large screen of a movie theater. If you begin to see an image, give yourself one point.

After completing all eight tasks, add the number of points you have accumulated. If you score between six and eight, consider yourself highly susceptible to hypnotic suggestion. A score of between three and five indicates moderate susceptibility. Scoring below two points indicates very low susceptibility.

If you find that you have scored low on this test, you may wish to retake it after a prolonged period of relaxation in a quiet, dark environment. This activity has been found to improve hypnotic susceptibility.

References

1. Introduction

Barber, T. X., Spanos, N. P., and Chaves, J. F. *Hypnotism, imagination, and human potentialities*. New York: Pergamon Press, 1974.

Conn, J. H., and Conn, R. N. Discussion of T. X. Barber's "Hypnosis as a causal variable in present-day psychology": A critical analysis. *International Journal of Clinical and Experimental Hypnosis*, 1967, *16*, 106-110.

Erickson, M. H. The applications of hypnosis to psychiatry. *Medical Record*, 1939, *150*, 60-65.

Erickson, M. H. *Advanced techniques of hypnosis and therapy*. New York: Grune and Stratton, 1967.

Fromm, E., and Shor, R. E. (Eds.). *Hypnosis: Research developments and perspectives*. Chicago: Aldine-Atherton, 1972.

Hilgard, E. R. *The experience of hypnosis*. New York: Harcourt, Brace, and World, 1965.

Hull, C. L. *Hypnosis and suggestibility: An experimental approach*. New York: Appleton-Century, 1933.

Orne, M. T. On the social psychology of the psychological experiment: With particular reference to demand characteristics and their implications. *American Psychologist*, 1962, *17*, 776-783.

Shor, R. E. The fundamental problem in hypnosis research as viewed from historic perspectives. In E. Fromm and R. E. Shor (Eds.), *Hypnosis: Research developments and perspectives*. Chicago: Aldine-Atherton, 1972.

Shor, R. E., and Orne, M. T. *The nature of hypnosis: Selected basic readings*. New York: Holt, Rinehart, and Winston, 1965.

2. Hypnotizability

Barber, T. X. *Hypnosis: A scientific approach.* Princeton, N.J.: Van Nostrand, 1969.

Barber, T. X., and Calverley, D. S. Hypnotic-like suggestibility in children and adults. *Journal of Abnormal and Social Psychology*, 1963, *66*, 589-597.

——— The definition of the situation as a variable affecting hypnotic-like suggestibility. *Journal of Clinical Psychology*, 1964, *20*, 438-440.

——— Empirical evidence for a theory of hypnotic behavior: Effects on suggestibility of five variables typically included in hypnotic induction procedures. *Journal of Consulting Psychology*, 1965, *29*, 98-107.

Barber, T. X., and Glass, L. B. Significant factors in hypnotic behavior. *Journal of Abnormal and Social Psychology*, 1962, *64*, 222-228.

Barber, T. X., Spanos, N. P., and Chaves, J. F. *Hypnotism, imagination, and human potentialities.* New York: Pergamon Press, 1974.

Bentler, P. M., and Hilgard, E. R. A comparison of group and individual induction of hypnosis with self-scoring and observer-scoring. *International Journal of Clinical and Experimental Hypnosis*, 1963, *11*, 49-54.

Borlone, M., Dittborn, J. M., and Palestrini, M. Correlaciones electroencefalograficas dentro de una definicion operacional de hipnosis somnambulica. *Acta Hipnologica Latinoamericana*, 1962, *1*, 9-19.

Cronin, D. M., Spanos, N. P., and Barber, T. X. Augmenting hypnotic suggestibility by providing favorable information about hypnosis. *American Journal of Clinical Hypnosis*, 1971, *13*, 259-264.

Diamond, M. J. The use of observationally presented information to modify hypnotic susceptibility. Unpublished doctoral dissertation, Stanford University, 1970.

——— Modification of hypnotizability: A review. *Psychological Bulletin*, 1974, *81*, 180-198.

Engstrom, D. R., London, P., and Hart, J. T. EEG alpha feedback training and hypnotic susceptibility. *Proceedings of the 78th Annual Convention of the American Psychological Association*, 1970, *5*, 837-838.

Gregory, J., and Diamond, M. J. Increasing hypnotic susceptibility by means of positive expectancies and written instruction. *Journal of Abnormal Psychology*, 1973, *82*, 363-367.

Hilgard, E. R. *Hypnotic susceptibility.* New York: Harcourt, Brace, and World, 1965.

Kramer, E. Hypnotic susceptibility and previous relationship with the hypnotist. *American Journal of Clinical Hypnosis*, 1969, *11*, 175-177.

Miller, R. J. Response to the Ponzo illusion as a reflection of hypnotic susceptibility. *International Journal of Clinical and Experimental Hypnosis*, 1975, *23*, 148-157.

Oswald, I. Experimental studies of rhythm, anxiety and cerebral vigilance. *Journal of Mental Science*, 1959, *105*, 269-294.

Pena, F. Perceptual isolation and hypnotic susceptibility. Unpublished doctoral dissertation, Washington State University, 1963.

Perry, C., Wilder, S., and Appignanesi, A. Hypnotic susceptibility and performance on a battery of creativity measures. *American Journal of Clinical Hypnosis*, 1973, *15*, 170-180.

Sanders, R. S., and Reyher, J. Sensory deprivation and the enhancement of hypnotic susceptibility. *Journal of Abnormal Psychology*, 1969, *74*, 375-381.

Shapiro, J. L., and Diamond, M. J. Increases in hypnotizability as a function of encounter group training: Some confirming evidence. *Journal of Abnormal Psychology*, 1972, *79*, 112-115.

Shor, R. E. Expectancies of being influenced and hypnotic performance. *International Journal of Clinical and Experimental Hypnosis*, 1971, *19*, 154-166.

Shor, R. E., and Orne, E. C. *The Harvard Group Scale of Hypnotic Susceptibility: Form A*. Palo Alto, Calif.: Consulting Psychologists Press, 1962.

Shor, R. E., and Schatz, J. A critical note on Barber's case study of J. *Journal of Psychology*, 1960, *50*, 253-256.

Sjoberg, B. M., and Hollister, L. E. The effects of psychotomimetic drugs on primary suggestibility. *Psychopharmacologia*, 1965, *8*, 251-262.

Spiegel, H. An eye-roll sign for hypnotizability. Paper read at the meeting of the Society for Clinical and Experimental Hypnosis, Philadelphia, 1970.

Sutcliffe, J. P., Perry, C. W., and Sheehan, P. W. Relation of some aspects of imagery and fantasy to hypnotic susceptibility. *Journal of Abnormal Psychology*, 1970, *76*, 279-287.

Tart, C. T. Psychedelic experiences associated with a novel procedure, mutual hypnosis. *American Journal of Clinical Hypnosis*, 1967, *10*, 65-78.

Ulett, G. A., Akpinar, S., and Itil, T. M. Hypnosis: Physiological, pharmacological reality. *American Journal of Psychiatry*, 1972, *128*, 33-39.

Wallace, B., and Garrett, J. B. Hypnotic susceptibility and autokinetic movement frequency. *Perceptual and Motor Skills*, 1973, *36*, 1054.

Wallace, B., Garrett, J. B., and Anstadt, S. P. Hypnotic susceptibility, suggestion, and reports of autokinetic movement. *American Journal of Psychology*, 1974, *87*, 117-123.

Wallace, B., Knight, T. A., and Garrett, J. B. Hypnotic susceptibility and frequency reports to illusory stimuli. *Journal of Abnormal Psychology*, 1976, *85*, 558-563.

Weitzenhoffer, A. M., and Hilgard, E. R. *Stanford Hypnotic Susceptibility Scale, Forms A and B*. Palo Alto, Calif.: Consulting Psychologists Press, 1959.

_____ *Stanford Hypnotic Susceptibility Scale, Form C*. Palo Alto, Calif.: Consulting Psychologists Press, 1962..

Wheeler, L., Reis, H. T., Wolff, E., Grupsmith, E., and Mordkoff, A. M. Eye-roll and hypnotic susceptibility. *International Journal of Clinical and Experimental Hypnosis*, 1974, *22*, 327-334.

Wickramasekera, I. The effects of sensory restriction on susceptibility to hypnosis: A hypothesis, some preliminary data, and theoretical speculation. *International Journal of Clinical and Experimental Hypnosis*, 1969, *17*, 217-224.

————. Effects of EMG feedback training on susceptibility to hypnosis: Preliminary observations. *Proceedings of the 79th Annual Convention of the American Psychological Association*, 1971, *6*, 783-784.

————. The effects of electromyographic feedback on hypnotic susceptibility: More preliminary data. *Journal of Abnormal Psychology*, 1973, *82*, 74-77.

Williams, G. W. Hypnosis in perspective. In L. M. LeCron (Ed.), *Experimental hypnosis*. New York: Macmillan, 1952.

Wilson, D. L. The role of confirmation of expectancies in hypnotic induction. Unpublished doctoral dissertation, University of North Carolina, 1967.

Zimbardo, P. G., Rapaport, C., and Baron, J. Pain control by hypnotic induction of motivational states. In P. G. Zimbardo (Ed.), *The cognitive control of motivation*. Glenview, Ill.: Scott, Foresman, 1969.

3. Hypnotherapy

Brenman, M., and Knight, R. P. Self-starvation and compulsive hopping with paradoxical reactions to hypnosis. *American Journal of Orthopsychiatry*, 1945, *15*, 65-75.

Cautela, J. R. The use of covert conditioning in hypnotherapy. *International Journal of Clinical and Experimental Hypnosis*, 1975, *23*, 15-27.

Coleman, J. C. *Abnormal psychology and modern life*. Fifth edition. Glenview, Ill.: Scott, Foresman, 1976.

Dengrove, E. *Hypnosis and behavior therapy*. Springfield, Ill.: Charles C. Thomas, 1976.

Donley, J. E. The clinical use of hypnoidization in the treatment of some functional psychoses. *Journal of Abnormal Psychology*, 1908, *3*, 148-160.

Kroger, W. S. Behavior modification and hypnotic conditioning in psychotherapy. In E. Dengrove (Ed.), *Hypnosis and behavior therapy*. Springfield, Ill.: Charles C. Thomas, 1976.

Lang, P. J., and Lazovik, A. D. Experimental desensitization of a phobia. *Journal of Abnormal and Social Psychology*, 1963, *66*, 519-525.

Lazarus, A. A. Sensory deprivation under hypnosis in the treatment of pervasive ("free-floating") anxiety: A preliminary impression. *South African Medical Journal*, 1963, *27*, 136.

Paterson, A. S. Acquisition of cortical control over autonomic malfunction in psychosomatic medicine through hypnosis. Paper presented at the meeting of the International Congress of Hypnosis and Psychosomatic Medicine, Kyoto, Japan, 1967.

Paul, G. L. *Insight versus desensitization in psychotherapy: An experiment in anxiety reduction*. Stanford, Calif.: Stanford University Press, 1966.

Platonov, K. I. *The word as a physiological and psychological factor*. Moscow: Foreign Language Publishing House, 1955.

Rothman, I., Carroll, M. L., and Rothman, F. D. Homework and self-hypnosis: The conditioning therapies in clinical practice. In E. Dengrove (Ed.), *Hypnosis and behavior therapy*. Springfield, Ill.: Charles C. Thomas, 1976.

Scott, D. L. Treatment of a severe phobia for birds by hypnosis. *American Journal of Clinical Hypnosis*, 1970, *12*, 146-149.

Spanos, N. P., DeMoor, W., and Barber, T. X. Hypnosis and behavior therapy: Common denominators. *American Journal of Clinical Hypnosis*, 1973, *16*, 45-64.

Wolpe, J. For phoria: A hair of the hound. *Psychology Today*, 1969, *3*, 34-37

4. Hypnotic Anesthesia and Analgesia

Anderson, M. N. Hypnosis in anesthesia. *Journal of the Medical Association of Alabama*, 1957, *27*, 121-125.

Andreychuck, T., and Skriver, C. Hypnosis and biofeedback in the treatment of migraine headaches. *International Journal of Clinical and Experimental Hypnosis*, 1975, *23*, 172-183.

August, R. V. Hypnosis in obstetrics: Varying approaches. *American Journal of Clinical Hypnosis*, 1965, *8*, 47-51.

Barber, T. X., and Calverley, D. S. Effect of E's tone of voice on hypnotic-like suggestibility. *Psychological Reports*, 1964, *15*, 139-144.

_____ Empirical evidence for a theory of hypnotic behavior: Effects on suggestibility of five variables typically included in hypnotic induction procedures. *Journal of Consulting Psychology*, 1965, *29*, 98-107 (a).

_____ Empirical evidence for a theory of hypnotic behavior: The suggestibility-enhancing effects of motivational suggestions, relaxation-sleep suggestions, and suggestions that the subjects will be effectively hypnotized. *Journal of Personality*, 1965, *33*, 256-270 (b).

_____ Toward a theory of hypnotic behavior: Experimental analyses of suggested amnesia. *Journal of Abnormal Psychology*, 1966, *71*, 95-107.

Barber, T. X., and DeMoor, W. A theory of hypnotic induction procedures. *American Journal of Clinical Hypnosis*, 1972, *15*, 112-135.

Davenport-Slack, B. A comparative evaluation of obstetrical hypnosis and antenatal childbirth training. *International Journal of Clinical and Experimental Hypnosis*, 1975, *23*, 266-281.

Davenport-Slack, B., and Boylan, C. H. Psychological correlates of childbirth pain. *Psychosomatic Medicine*, 1974, *36*, 215-222.

Esdaile, J. *Hypnosis in medicine and surgery.* New York: Julian Press, 1957. (Original date of publication: 1850)

Garrett, J. B., and Bloom, E. The relation between hypnotic induction modality and authoritarianism. Paper read at the annual meeting of the Society of Clinical and Experimental Hypnosis, Chicago, 1975.

Garrett, J. B., and Wallace, B. A novel test of hypnotic anesthesia. *International Journal of Clinical and Experimental Hypnosis*, 1975, *23*, 139-147.

Graham, G. W. Hypnotic treatment for migraine headaches. *International Journal of Clinical and Experimental Hypnosis*, 1975, *23*, 165-171.

Hilgard, E. R., and Hilgard, J. R. *Hypnosis in the relief of pain.* Los Altos, Calif.: Kaufmann, 1975.

Huttel, F. A., Mitchell, I., Fischer, W. M., and Meyer, A. E. A quantitative evaluation of psychoprophylaxis in childbirth. *Journal of Psychosomatic Research*, 1972, *16*, 81-92.

Jacobson, E. *How to relax and have your baby: Scientific relaxation in childbirth.* New York: McGraw-Hill, 1959.

Javert, C. T., and Hardy, J. D. Influence of analgesics on pain intensity during labor (with a note on "natural childbirth"). *Anesthesiology*, 1951, *12*, 189-215.

Kroger, W. S. *Childbirth with hypnosis*. Garden City, N.Y.: Doubleday, 1961.

————. *Clinical and experimental hypnosis in medicine, dentistry, and psychology*. Philadelphia: Lippincott, 1963.

Miller, H. L. Education for childbirth. *Obstetrics and Gynecology*, 1961, *17*, 120-123.

Moss, A. A. Hypnodontics: Hypnosis in dentistry. In W. S. Kroger, *Clinical and experimental hypnosis in medicine, dentistry, and psychology*. Philadelphia: Lippincott, 1963.

Pascatto, R. D., and Mead, B. T. The use of posthypnotic suggestion in obstetrics. *American Journal of Clinical Hypnosis*, 1967, *9*, 267-268.

Pulver, S. E., and Pulver, M. P. Hypnosis in medical and dental practice: A survey. *International Journal of Clinical and Experimental Hypnosis*, 1975, *23*, 28-47.

Ringrose, C. A. D. Autohypnosis as an adjunct in obstetrics. *Medical Trial Technology Quarterly*, 1966, *13*, 21-28.

Sargent, J. D., Green, E. E., and Walters, E. D. Preliminary report on the use of autogenic feedback training in the treatment of migraine and tension headaches. *Psychosomatic Medicine*, 1973, *35*, 129-135.

Spanos, N. P. Goal-directed fantasy and the performance of hypnotic test suggestions. *Psychiatry*, 1971, *34*, 86-96.

Tanzer, D. The psychology of pregnancy and childbirth: An investigation of natural childbirth. Unpublished doctoral dissertation, Brandeis University, 1967.

Tom, K. S. Hypnosis in obstetrics and gynecology. *Obstetrics and Gynecology*, 1960, *16*, 222-225.

Wallace, B. Immediate proprioceptive decrement with hypnotic anesthesia: A preliminary report. *Perceptual and Motor Skills*, 1976, *42*, 801-802.

Wallace, B., and Garrett, J. B. Reduced felt arm sensation effects on visual adaptation. *Perception and Psychophysics*, 1973, *14*, 597-600.

————. Perceptual adaptation with selective reductions of felt sensation. *Perception*, 1975, *4*, 437-445.

5. Sexual Dysfunction and Hypnosis

Coleman, J. C. *Abnormal psychology and modern life*. Fifth edition. Glenview, Ill.: Scott, Foresman, 1976.

Erickson, M. H. Psychotherapy achieved by a reversal of the neurotic processes in a case of ejaculatio precox. *American Journal of Clinical Hypnosis*, 1973, *15*, 217-222.

Fuchs, K., Hoch, Z., and Kleinhauz, M. Hypno-desensitization therapy of vaginismus. Paper read at the International Congress of Hypnosis and Psychosomatic Medicine, Philadelphia, 1976.

Fuchs, K., Hoch, Z., Paldi, E., Abramovici, H., Brandes, J. M., Timor-Tritsch, I., and Kleinhauz, M. Hypno-desensitization therapy of vaginismus: Part I.

"In vitro" method. Part II. "In vivo" method. *International Journal of Clinical and Experimental Hypnosis,* 1973, *21,* 144-156.

Kaplan, H. S. No-nonsense therapy for six sexual malfunctions. *Psychology Today,* 1974, *8,* 76-80, 83-84, 86.

——————. *The illustrated manual of sex therapy.* New York: Quadrangle/The New York Times Book Company, 1975.

Masters, W. H., and Johnson, V. E. *Human sexual inadequacy.* Boston: Little, Brown, 1970.

——————. *The pleasure bond: A new look at sexuality and commitment.* Boston: Little, Brown, 1975.

Nuland, W. The use of hypnosis in the treatment of impotence. Paper read at the International Congress of Hypnosis and Psychosomatic Medicine, Philadelphia, 1976.

Segal, H. J. Psychotherapy vs. hypnotherapy in the treatment of sex problems. *American Journal of Clinical Hypnosis,* 1970, *13,* 128-130.

Wickramasekera, I. Personal communication, 1976.

6. Habit Control

Beahrs, J. O., and Hill, M. M. Treatment of alcoholism by group-interaction psychotherapy under hypnosis. *American Journal of Clinical Hypnosis,* 1971, *14,* 60-62.

Bernstein, D. A. Modification of smoking behavior: An evaluative review. *Psychological Bulletin,* 1969, *71,* 418-440.

Byers, A. P. Training and use of technicians in the treatment of alcoholism with hypnosis. *American Journal of Clinical Hypnosis,* 1975, *18,* 90-93.

Dengrove, E. A single-treatment method to stop smoking using ancillary self-hypnosis: Discussion. *International Journal of Clinical and Experimental Hypnosis,* 1970, *18,* 251-256.

Erickson, M. H. The utilization of patient therapy in the hypnotherapy of obesity: Three case reports. *American Journal of Clinical Hypnosis,* 1960, *3,* 112-116.

Hall, J. A., and Crasilneck, H. B. Development of a hypnotic technique for treating chronic cigarette smoking. *International Journal of Clinical and Experi-mental Hypnosis,* 1970, *18,* 283-289.

Kennedy, W. A., and Foreyt, J. Control of eating behavior in an obese patient by avoidance conditioning. *Psychological Reports,* 1968, *22,* 571-576.

Kroger, W. S. The conditioned reflex treatment of alcoholism. *Journal of the American Medical Association,* 1942, *120,* 714.

——————. *Clinical and experimental hypnosis in medicine, dentistry, and psychology.* Philadelphia: Lippincott, 1963.

——————. Systems approach for understanding obesity: Management by behavior modification through hypnosis. *Psychiatric Opinion,* 1970, *7,* 7-19.

Mikulus, W. L. *Behavior modification: An overview.* New York: Harper and Row, 1972.

Platonov, K. I. *The word as a physiological and therapeutic factor.* Moscow: Foreign Language Publishing House, 1955.

Spiegel, H. A single-treatment method to stop smoking using ancillary self-hypnosis. *International Journal of Clinical and Experimental Hypnosis*, 1970, *18*, 235-250.

Stuart, R. B. Behavior control of overeating. *Behavior Research and Therapy*, 1967, *5*, 357-365.

———. A three-dimensional program for the treatment of obesity. *Behavior Research and Therapy*, 1971, *9*, 177-186.

Stunkard, A. J. The management of obesity. *New York Journal of Medicine*, 1958, *58*, 79-87.

———. Behavior modification of obesity and anorexia nervosa. In N. Kiell (Ed.), *The psychology of obesity*, Springfield, Ill.: Charles C. Thomas, 1973.

Stunkard, A. J., and McLaren-Hume, M. The results of treatment for obesity. *Archives of Internal Medicine*, 1959, *103*, 79-85.

Wallerstein, R. S. *Hospital treatment of alcoholism*. New York: Basic Books, 1958.

Wolpe, J. *The practice of behavior therapy*. New York: Pergamon Press, 1969.

7. Information Processing and Hypnosis

Ascher, L. M., Barber, T. X., and Spanos, N. P. Two attempts to replicate the Parrish-Lundy-Leibowitz experiment on hypnotic age regression. *American Journal of Clinical Hypnosis*, 1972, *14*, 178-185.

Barber, T. X. Experimental evidence for a theory of hypnotic behavior: II. Experimental controls in hypnotic age regression. *International Journal of Clinical and Experimental Hypnosis*, 1961, *9*, 181-193.

———. Hypnotic age regression: A critical review. *Psychosomatic Medicine*, 1962, *24*, 286-299.

Barber, T. X., Spanos, N. P., and Chaves, J. F. *Hypnotism, imagination, and human potentialities*. New York: Pergamon Press, 1974.

Fisher, S. Problems of interpretation and controls in hypnotic research. In G. H. Estabrooks (Ed.), *Hypnosis: Current problems*. New York: Harper and Row, 1962.

Garrett, J. B. Unpublished research, 1974.

———. Effect of hypnotic time distortion upon embedded figures test performance. Paper read at the meeting of the American Psychological Association, Chicago, 1975.

———. Personal communication, 1976.

Graham, C., and Leibowitz, H. W. The effect of suggestion on visual acuity. *International Journal of Clinical and Experimental Hypnosis*, 1972, *20*, 169-186.

Haber, R. N., and Haber, R. B. Eidetic imagery: I. Frequency. *Perceptual and Motor Skills*, 1964, *19*, 131-138.

Harwood, L. R. Changes in visual acuity in myopic subjects which are similar to those in hypnotized myopic subjects. Paper read at the meeting of the American Academy of Optometry, Toronto, 1971.

Krauss, H. H., Katzell, R., and Krauss, B. J. Effect of hypnotic time distortion upon free-recall learning. *Journal of Abnormal Psychology*, 1974, *83*, 140-144.

O'Connell, D. N., Shor, R. E., and Orne, M. T. Hypnotic age regression: An empirical and methodological analysis. *Journal of Abnormal Psychology Monograph Supplement*, 1970, *76*, No. 3, Part 2, 1-32.

Parrish, M., Lundy, R. M., and Leibowitz, H. W. Effect of hypnotic age regression on the magnitude of the Ponzo and Poggendorff illusions. *Journal of Abnormal Psychology*, 1969, *74*, 693-698.

Porter, J., Woodward, J., Bisbee, C., and Fenker, R. Effect of hypnotic age regression on the magnitude of the Ponzo illusion. *Journal of Abnormal Psychology*, 1972, *79*, 189-194.

True, R. M. Experimental control in hypnotic age regression states. *Science*, 1949. *110*, 583-584.

Walker, N. S., Garrett, J. B., and Wallace, B. Restoration of eidetic imagery via hypnotic age regression: A preliminary report. *Journal of Abnormal Psychology*, 1976, *85*, 335-337.

Zimbardo, P. G., Marshall, G., White, G., and Maslach, C. Objective assessment of hypnotically induced time distortion. *Science*, 1973, *181*, 282-284.

8. Hypnosis, Sleep, Dreams and ESP

Aserinsky, E., and Kleitman, N. Regularly occurring period of eye motility, and concomitant phenomena, during sleep. *Science*, 1953, *118*, 273-274.

Beloff, J., and Mandelberg, I. An attempted validation of the Ryzl technique for training ESP subjects. *Journal of the Society for Psychical Research*, 1966, *43*, 229-249.

Brady, J. P., and Rosner, B. S. Rapid eye movements in hypnotically induced dreams. *Journal of Nervous and Mental Diseases*, 1966, *143*, 28-35.

Casler, L. The improvement of clairvoyance scores by means of hypnotic suggestion. *Journal of Parapsychology*, 1962, *26*, 77-87.

——— Self-generated hypnotic suggestions and clairvoyance. *International Journal of Parapsychology*, 1967, *9*, 125-128.

Chertok, L., and Kramarz, P. Hypnosis, sleep, and electroencephalography. *Journal of Nervous and Mental Diseases*, 1959, *128*, 227-238.

Evans, F. J. Hypnosis and sleep: Techniques for exploring cognitive activity during sleep. In E. Fromm and R. E. Shor (Eds.), *Hypnosis: Research developments and perspectives*. Chicago: Aldine-Atherton, 1972.

Evans, F. J., Gustafson, L. A., O'Connell, D. N., Orne, M. T., and Shor, R. E. Sleep-induced behavioral response: Relationship to susceptibility to hypnosis and laboratory sleep patterns. *Journal of Nervous and Mental Diseases, 1969, 148*, 467-476.

Evans, F. J., Reich, L. H., and Orne, M. T. Optokinetic nystagmus, eye movements, and hypnotically induced hallucinations. *Journal of Nervous and Mental Diseases*, 1972, *152*, 419-431.

Fahler, J., and Cadoret, R. J. ESP card tests of college students with and without hypnosis. *Journal of Parapsychology*, 1958, *22*, 125-136.

Galbraith, G. C., London, P., Leibovitz, M. P., Cooper, L. M. and Hart. J. T. EEG and hypnotic susceptibility. *Journal of Comparative and Physiological Psychology*, 1970, *72*, 125-131.

Grela, J. J. Effect on ESP scoring of hypnotically induced attitudes. *Journal of Parapsychology*, 1945, *9*, 194-202.

Halper, C., Pivik, T., and Dement, W. An attempt to reduce the REM rebound following REM deprivation by the use of induced waking mentation. Paper presented at the meeting of the Association for the Psychophysiological Study of Sleep, Boston, 1969.

Honorton, C. Significant factors in hypnotically induced clairvoyant dreams. *Journal of the American Society for Psychical Research*, 1972, *66*, 86-102.

Honorton, C., and Krippner, S. Hypnosis and ESP performance: A review of the experimental literature. *Journal of the American Society for Psychical Research*, 1969, *63*, 214-253.

Honorton, C., and Stump, J. P. A preliminary study of hypnotically induced clairvoyant dreams. *Journal of the American Society for Psychical Research*, 1969, *63*, 175-184.

Jakobson, A., and Kales, A. Somnambulism: All night EEG and related studies. In S. S. Kety, E. V. Evarts, and H. L. Williams (Eds.), *Sleep and altered states of consciousness*. Baltimore: Williams and Wilkins, 1965.

Kamiya, J. Operant control of the EEG alpha rhythm and some of its reported effects on consciousness. In C. T. Tart (Ed.), *Altered states of consciousness*. New York: Wiley, 1969.

Krippner, S. Experimentally induced telepathic effects in hypnosis and non-hypnosis groups. *Journal of the American Society for Psychical Research*, 1968, *62*, 387-398.

London, P., Hart, J. T., and Leibovitz, M. P. EEG alpha rhythms and susceptibility to hypnosis. *Nature*, 1968, *219*, 71-72.

Merenina, A. I. Further investigation of the dynamics of cerebral potentials in the various phases of hypnosis in man. *Fiziologicheskii Zhurnal SSSR imeni I. M. Sechenova*, 1955, *41*, 742-747.

Rhine, J. B. Hypnotic suggestion in PK tests. *Journal of Parapsychology*, 1946, *10*, 126-140.

Ryzl, M. Training the psi faculty by hypnosis. *Journal of the Society of Psychical Research*, 1962, *41*, 234-252.

————. A method of training in ESP. *International Journal of Parapsychology*, 1966, *8*, 501-532.

Ryzl, M., and Ryzlova, J. A case of high-scoring ESP performance in the hypnotic state. *Journal of Parapsychology*, 1962, *26*, 153-171.

Simon, C. W., and Emmons, W. H. EEG, consciousness, and sleep. *Science*, 1956, *124*, 1066-1069.

Stoyva, J. M. Posthypnotically suggested dreams and the sleep cycle. *Archives of General Psychiatry*, 1965, *12*, 287-294.

Tart, C. T. The hypnotic dream: Methodological problems and a review of the literature. *Psychological Bulletin*, 1965, *63*, 87-99.

————. Waking from sleep at a preselected time. *Journal of the American Society of Psychosomatic Dentistry and Medicine*, 1970, *17*, 3-16.

9. Stage Hypnosis

Anderson, M. L., and Sarbin, T. R. Base rate expectancies and motoric alterations in hypnosis. *International Journal of Clinical and Experimental Hypnosis*, 1964, *12*, 147-158.

Barber, T. X. *Hypnosis: A scientific approach.* New York: Van Nostrand Reinhold, 1969.

Barber, T. X., and Calverley, D. S. Toward a theory of hypnotic behavior: Effects on suggestibility of defining the situation as hypnosis and defining response to suggestions as easy. *Journal of Abnormal and Social Psychology,* 1964, *68,* 585-592.

————. Empirical evidence for a theory of hypnotic behavior: Effects on suggestibility of five variables typically included in hypnotic induction procedures. *Journal of Consulting Psychology,* 1965, *29,* 98-107.

Barber, T. X., Spanos, N. P., and Chaves, J. F. *Hypnotism, imagination and human potentialities.* New York: Pergamon Press, 1974.

Brandon, J. *Successful hypnotism.* New York: Stravon, 1956.

Ganong, W. F. *Review of medical physiology.* Los Altos, Calif.: Lange Medical Publications, 1967.

Meeker, W., and Barber, T. X. Toward an explanation of stage hypnosis. *Journal of Abnormal Psychology,* 1971, *77,* 61-70.

Orne, M. T. Antisocial behavior and hypnosis: Problems of control and validation in empirical studies. In G. H. Estabrooks (Ed.), *Hypnosis: Current problems.* New York: Harper and Row, 1962.

Tracy, D. F. *Hypnosis.* New York: Sterling Publishing Co., 1952.

Whitlow, J. A. A rapid method for the induction of hypnosis. In L. M. LeCron (Ed.), *Experimental hypnosis.* New York: Macmillan, 1948.

10. The Future of Hypnosis

Fromm, E. Quo vadis hypnosis? Predictions of future trends in hypnosis research. In E. Fromm and R. E. Shor (Eds.), *Hypnosis: Research developments and perspectives.* Chicago: Aldine-Atherton, 1972.

Garrett, J. B. Personal communication, 1972.

AUTHOR INDEX

SUBJECT INDEX

4

4

1994